English Matters!

Series Consultant
WILLIAM STRONG, Ph.D.
Department Head and Professor of Secondary Education
Director, Utah Writing Project
Utah State University

Advisers
BEVERLY ANN CHIN, Ph.D.
Former President of National Council of Teachers of English and
Professor of English
University of Montana

MARILEE FOGLESONG
Former Young Adult Coordinator
New York Public Library

Volume 2
book report – conferencing

GROLIER
EDUCATIONAL

SHERMAN TURNPIKE, DANBURY, CONNECTICUT 06816

Published 2000 by Grolier Educational
Sherman Turnpike
Danbury, CT 06816

Developed, Designed, and Produced by BOOK BUILDERS INCORPORATED
Cover design: Sherry Williams
Cover photography: Tilman Reitzle

SET ISBN: 0-7172-9437-4
VOLUME ISBN: 0-7172-9439-0

For information address the publisher:
Grolier Educational, Sherman Turnpike, Danbury, CT 06816

Library of Congress Cataloging-in-Publication Data

English matters!
     p. cm.
   Includes index.
   SUMMARY: A multi-volume English language textbook with alphabetically arranged entries on such topics as grammar, style, punctuation, and writing and research skills.
   ISBN 0-7172-9437-4 (set : alk. paper)
   1. English language—Rhetoric Handbooks, manuals, etc. 2. English language—Grammar Handbooks, manuals, etc. 3. English language—Usage Handbooks, manuals, etc. 4. Report writing Handbooks, manuals, etc. [1. English language—Rhetoric. 2. English language—Grammar. 3. English language—Usage. 4. Report writing.] I. Grolier Educational (Firm)
PE1408 .E52 1999
428.2'4 —dc21
                                                                                          99-33249
                                                                                               CIP

Contents

Preface

The Purpose of *English Matters!*

Welcome to *English Matters!*—the one encyclopedia that helps with just about any matter you come across in English or language-arts classes, assignments, and tests. The ten-volume set sends you on your way to finding answers to questions about writing and speaking style, grammar, usage, and punctuation. Whatever question you have about English, you are likely to find the answer in *English Matters!*

Here are some example questions:

- SPELLING AND VOCABULARY: What's the **plural** of *potato*? of *patio*?
- WORDS COMMONLY CONFUSED: Should I write *affect* or *effect*?
- MECHANICS AND PUNCTUATION: Do I use two **punctuation** marks after this **abbreviation**?
- GRAMMAR AND USAGE: What does "**fragment**" written next to my sentence mean?
- PARTS OF SPEECH: What's a **relative pronoun** relative to?
- WRITING: What will make my **paragraph** of **description** more descriptive?
- THINKING SKILLS: Is a **logical jump** something good or something bad?
- LITERARY TERMS: How are **sonnets** different from other poems?
- SPEAKING/LISTENING: Where can I find how to perform **readers' theater**?
- RESEARCH: How do I make a **bibliography** for my paper?
- TEST-TAKING: Where can I find out about **college-entrance tests**?

Use *English Matters!* to look up any of the dark, or boldfaced, words from the list of questions, and you will find the answers.

Looking Things Up

Each boldfaced term from the preceding list is called a **key word**. The key words appear in alphabetical order, A to Z, in the appropriate volume of *English Matters!* and in the set index at the back of each of the ten vol-umes. Alongside each key word in the ten volumes, you will find either an entry—definition, simple explanation, and lots of examples—or a cross-reference to an alternative key word and entry.

The pages with blue side borders call attention to the most important key words, to those that are the building blocks for everything you do with English. To be successful in life, you need to know the meaning of these terms—and how to follow, bend, and even break the rules related to them. For example, you need to know when you *must* use a comma and when the choice is up to you, when you should not split an infinitive and when it is okay to do so.

Although rules are important, the more than one thousand entries in *English Matters!* go beyond the rules of English. You'll find helpful examples of concepts like **noun** and **narrative**. And you'll find interesting graphics—everything from the layout for a **business letter** to illustrations of a **pie chart** and a **Venn diagram**.

In the margins are useful boxes of at-a-glance information: **Checklist** summarizes steps in a process; **Helpful Hint** short-circuits errors; **Memory Jogger** distinguishes homonyms; **Net Source** helps to locate reliable Internet sites; **Punctuation Pointer** reinforces the mechanics of writing; and **Word Check** will help increase your vocabulary. One more feature—**For Further Reading**—suggests other sources of interest to students your age.

Our cross-referencing of key words makes your research easier by showing you how interconnected hundreds of terms are. The cross-references appear in small capitalized type, either in the entry itself (as for the term QUOTATION in the entry for **capitalization**) or in the margin under the label *See also* (as for the term SPELLING in the entry for **comparative degree**).

English Matters! offers you the engaging facts and practical advice to help you do well in what really matters—your professional and personal future. We encourage you to ask questions often and to turn to *English Matters!* for answers.

William Strong, Ph.D.
Series Consultant

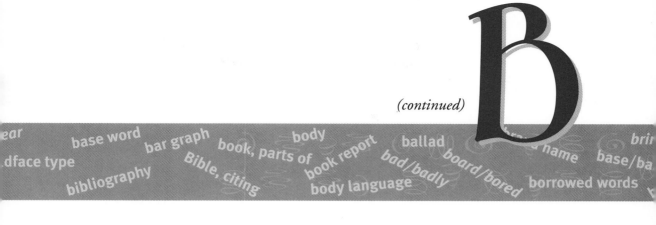

ear base word bar graph book, parts of body book report ballad name brir
dface type Bible, citing body language bad/badly board/bored base/ba
bibliography borrowed words

book report An ESSAY or ORAL PRESENTATION that is typically assigned in school to give students an opportunity to comment on a book they have read outside class and to share their response with both the teacher and their classmates.

When you prepare a book report, assume that your AUDIENCE has not read the book itself. Provide a brief SUMMARY of the main points or events, and for a work of FICTION introduce your audience to the main CHARACTERS and their concerns.

An effective book report also offers an evaluation so that your readers can decide if they would like to read the book themselves.

- Did the book capture your interest and hold it to the end? Tell your readers about two or three specific aspects that made the book compelling.
- Were you disappointed in the book? Tell your readers about its shortcomings.

If you are presenting your book report orally, consider using a visual aid such as the book itself, an illustration, or a poster to add further interest. Your listeners may also appreciate knowing about other books by the same author if the book you are presenting is one you enjoyed and are recommending.

See also
BOOK REVIEW
BOOKTALK

See also

BOOK REPORT

BOOKTALK

≡≡Net Source≡≡

On-line sites offering more balanced (and less promotional) analyses of books include <http://scholar.lib.vt.edu/ejournals/ALAN/alan-review.html>, <http://www.ala.org/booklist/index.html>, and <http://www.nytimes .com>.

See also

BOOK REPORT

BOOK REVIEW

ORAL PRESENTATION

≡≡Net Source≡≡

Explore *Nancy Keane's Booktalks—Quick and Simple* at <www.concord.k12.nh.us/schools/rundlett/booktalks>.

book review A critical ANALYSIS, typically written shortly after the publication of a book. Book reviews may appear in newspapers, in magazines, or on-line. Judgmental by nature, the classic book review focuses on a work's strengths and weaknesses; it attempts to evaluate the book's potential place in literary history. Often it discusses the book under consideration in the context of the AUTHOR's other works (if any) or contemporary literary developments.

On-line bookstores post their own book reviews to entice potential readers (and buyers). Sites such as <barnesandnoble.com> and <amazon.com> provide a wealth of book reviews, some of which they write. While such reviews are informative and useful, you must remember they are promotional—that is, advertising meant to persuade you to buy the book (see ADVERTISING, TECHNIQUES OF).

booktalk A brief book promotion designed to interest readers. Booktalks are commonly given by librarians or teachers helping students choose books to read but can be given by students sharing their reading with classmates. Many people planning booktalks purposely have more books available than they can present at once. With the books attractively displayed, they ask listeners which books they would like to hear about.

Some presenters group books by topic, providing students with choices around a common THEME (for example, dog books such as *Shiloh* by Phyllis Reynolds Naylor, *Sounder* by William H. Armstrong, and *Grey King* by Susan Cooper).

Typically, a booktalk provides a brief SUMMARY of the PLOT or mentions one part of the plot and goes on to identify readers who might find the book particularly interesting (for example, SCIENCE FICTION enthusiasts or MYSTERY readers). In addition, a booktalk may include an oral reading of a passage that will engage prospective readers and give them a feeling for the text. Effective booktalks are provocative, designed to make listeners want to read the book to find out how the main CHARACTER resolves a dilemma, but never give away the ending.

For Further Reading

Useful books on or about booktalks include *Books Kids Will Sit Still For* and *More Books Kids Will Sit Still For,* both by Judy Freeman, and Joni Bodart's *Booktalk!* volumes 1–5.

book title The name of a book. In addition to the main title the work may have a SUBTITLE. When you refer to a book, use a COLON between the title and the subtitle, even if no colon appears there on the book's cover or title page (see BOOK, PARTS OF).

MAIN TITLE   SUBTITLE
Mythology: The Voyage of the Hero

Capitalize the first letters of the first and last words and all other important words in a title and subtitle (see CAPITALIZATION). Usually, you don't need to capitalize a PREPOSITION, but check with your teacher. Use ITALICS (or underlining) for titles of books and other long works.

Boolean search A means of searching for information in an electronic DATABASE. The search system is named for the nineteenth-century English mathematician George Boole, who developed formulas that help researchers in the twenty-first century. His method provides a way of stating exactly what information you want software to find for you and what you don't want it to find.

See also
BIBLIOGRAPHY
TITLE, OF WORK
WORKS-CITED LIST

— Helpful Hint — ☞

More Search Advice

Some search engines allow you to use SYMBOLS.

python + habitat

python − Monty

To specify that the entire phrase must appear exactly as you have typed it, enclose it in QUOTATION MARKS.

"endangered habitat"

See also

ASIAN LANGUAGES, INFLUENCE ON ENGLISH

CELTIC LANGUAGES, INFLUENCE ON ENGLISH

DUTCH, INFLUENCE ON ENGLISH

LATIN, INFLUENCE ON ENGLISH

and other languages

The Boolean method of searching is widely (but not exclusively) used on the Internet. It allows you to tell a SEARCH ENGINE to find sites that contain one or more KEYWORDS.

If you want to find a site that contains *either* of two or more keywords, you can type

python habitat

or

python OR habitat

To specify that both words *must* appear in the search results, type

python AND habitat

To specify that a word must *not* appear in the search results, type

python NOT Monty

borrowed words Words brought into one language from another. Many of the words we use daily were "borrowed" (never to be returned) centuries ago; we don't think of them as foreign words at all. *Café,* for example, came into English from FRENCH.

Words enter a language for a variety of reasons, the most important being proximity. Speakers must hear foreign words frequently in order to borrow them. Exposure has tended to take these forms:

- Being conquered by a foreign power. When England fell to invading Germanic and Norse tribes, English gained words from GERMANIC LANGUAGES and from Old Norse. Many of the words we take for granted as English entered the language from French and LATIN after the Norman Conquest of 1066.

- Trading with foreign lands. As English explorers traveled the world, chiefly in the fifteenth to nineteenth centuries, words from ARABIC, Sanskrit, Chinese, and so forth came into the language. The word *ketchup,* for example, entered English from Chinese. Constant commerce and political interaction with other European nations also brought words from French, SPANISH, ITALIAN, GERMAN, and GREEK into English.

English also absorbs words from other languages for these reasons:

- The foreign language has a word for something previously unnamed in English. For example, English explorers of the Americas adopted *mosquito* from Spanish in the 1500s to name an insect new to them. Conversely, English commonly "lends" technology words, such as *software,* to other languages.
- English speakers study a foreign language and incorporate its words into their English speech from a desire to appear sophisticated. For instance, some people prefer to use the French term *savoir faire* to refer to an ability to do just the right thing.

brace A SYMBOL used, usually in a CHART or TABLE, to indicate that certain words or numbers are to be considered as a group. Braces are sometimes referred to as curly BRACKETS. A large single brace may be typeset or handwritten next to several lines of information to show that those lines go together.

 Use one of these marks at the end of a sentence.

Use one of these marks between main clauses of a sentence.

bracket One of a pair of typographical marks—[ ]—used to enclose information that needs to be set aside from the rest of the text. For example, brackets enclose the word SIC in a QUOTATION to indicate that even though what is written looks wrong, the quotation is accurate. Brackets also enclose any other explanation a writer inserts into a quotation.

> Lincoln said, "Four score and seven [87] years ago, our fathers brought forth on this continent, a new nation...."

Brackets are used to create PARENTHESES within parentheses to avoid confusion.

> Meditation and frequent vacations may relieve stress. (As Wordsworth says, "The world is too much with us" [1807].)

See also

CLUSTERING
LISTING
LOOPING

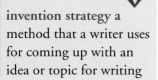

Word Check ✔

invention strategy a method that a writer uses for coming up with an idea or topic for writing

brainstorming An invention strategy (see PREWRITING) that uses the brain's power of association to generate ideas. Brainstorming is particularly useful when you are just beginning to write a paper, solve a problem, or work on a project.

There are many ways to brainstorm. You can brainstorm alone or in a group. Brainstorming can result in LISTS; in FREEWRITING, where your ideas are recorded in PROSE; or in visual representations of your thinking (see MAPPING). Whatever form you choose to record your brainstorming, you do need to keep three key ideas in mind:

1. Use written language. Brainstorming works because language both generates and enables thought. Thought both generates thought and enables thought to generate language. In other words, you think to write and write to think. In addition, writing allows you to keep a permanent record of all your ideas so that you can go back and edit them later.

2. Accept every idea, even if it seems far-fetched or silly. Often, an idea that is off target generates another idea that works very well. Work quickly and steadily, jotting down every idea in whatever manner will allow you to remember it later. At this point it is better to get down many ideas than to pause and develop a single idea. Don't concern yourself with SPELLING, PUNCTUATION, or GRAMMAR AND USAGE. Consider your brainstorming as private writing or notes to yourself.

When brainstorming in a group, you may wish to adopt a model from the business world: ask one member of the group to act as recorder, listing on a whiteboard or overhead slide all ideas offered.

3. Brainstorming takes time. Most people feel that brainstorming takes at least ten to fifteen minutes. During the first few minutes you will typically find yourself listing obvious ideas. Your really good ideas may come after you've warmed up or think that you can't think of anything else. Trust your brain, and push yourself a little. You will be surprised with what you come up with.

brake/break *Brake* refers to a device for stopping or to the act of stopping.

> Use your brake at the red light.
> Please brake for pedestrians.

Break refers to separating something into more pieces than before or making an object unusable. It also refers to taking a rest in the middle of something and to a split or division.

> Don't break the dishes.
> Let's take a break from homework and play volley-
> ball.
> We'll buy popcorn when there's a break at halftime.

See also

BUSINESS, NAME OF

brand name The name of a specific product. Capitalize the first letter of a brand name (see CAPITALIZATION). Brand names may be made-up words or unusual arrangements of existing words.

Some brand names include a capital letter—or intercap—with no space between words.

> RollerBlade

Do not use a brand name as a COMMON NOUN or as a substitute for "a product such as."

> NOT: I need a Kleenex.
> BUT: I need a tissue.

> NOT: Make a Xerox of your research paper.
> BUT: Make a photocopy of your research paper.

breath/breathe *Breath* is a NOUN; *breathe* is a VERB. The *e* on the end of the verb tells you to pronounce the middle vowels as long *e* and to pronounce the *th* as in the word *the*.

bring/take Both *bring* and *take* refer to transporting something from one place to another. Use *bring* to refer to transporting something to the speaker.

> Please bring me a drink of water.

Use *take* to refer to transporting something *away from* the speaker.

> Please take this note to your teacher.

> **— Helpful Hint —**
> ☞
> **Bring/Come;**
> **Take/Go**
> *Come* and *bring* indicate movement toward the speaker; *go* and *take* indicate movement away from the speaker.

British English, influence on American English British English is the English language as it is spoken and written in Great Britain. The STANDARD ENGLISH used in the United States is American English, and it differs in some ways from British English. You may need to use British English when writing DIALOGUE for a British CHARACTER. But in general use American English in American schools.

British settlers in America brought the English language along with them, making it the dominant language in the colonies. Settlers soon added new words to describe new animals, plants, and landscapes. They BORROWED WORDS such as *raccoon* from Native Americans and also took words from other European languages such as DUTCH, German [see GERMANIC LANGUAGES], FRENCH, and SPANISH.

The American author Noah Webster (1758–1843) began to collect words used by educated Americans.

See also
ACCENT (DIALECT)
ASIAN LANGUAGES, INFLUENCE ON ENGLISH
CELTIC LANGUAGES, INFLUENCE ON ENGLISH
LATIN, INFLUENCE ON ENGLISH
MODERN ENGLISH
and other languages

Some were new words. Some were old words that were pronounced or spelled differently from the way they were pronounced or spelled in Great Britain. Others were old words that had been given new meanings. Webster published the *American Dictionary of the English Language,* based on his research, in 1828 (see DICTIONARY).

Today, American and British English are actually growing more alike. Influenced by the exchange of movies, radio and television programs, and recorded vocal music, the two versions of English resemble each other more than they did a hundred or so years ago. Nevertheless, there are still some differences.

Differences in Spelling

Many words that end in *or* in American English end with *our* in British English. Words that end in *er* in American English may end in *re* in the British version. Other variations in SPELLING are not so easily classified.

AMERICAN	BRITISH
tire	tyre
gray	grey

Differences in Vocabulary

Quite different American and British words may mean the same thing.

AMERICAN	BRITISH
apartment	flat
backpack	rucksack
diaper	nappy
doctor's office	surgery

Net Source

For a dictionary of British English, see <http://pages.prodigy.com/NY/NYC/britspk/main.html>. For more on some differences in spelling and vocabulary, see <http://www.scrit.wlv.ac.uk/wwlib/american.html>.

browser *See* BOOLEAN SEARCH; COMPUTER; INTERNET; WORLD WIDE WEB

building, structure Capitalize names of buildings or structures (see CAPITALIZATION). Don't capitalize *the* before names, and don't capitalize a generic part of the name such as *building* or *palace* when it stands alone.

> the <u>Sears Tower</u>, but the <u>tower</u>
> the <u>Golden Gate Bridge</u>, but the <u>bridge</u>

bullet Typographical SYMBOL preceding each item in a LIST, used for the purpose of making the list stand out or helping readers see where a new list item begins. Most word-processing programs offer several bullet options and automatically begin a new item on a list with a bullet if you activate the bullet button or command. The most common bullet is a simple, centered dot [•], but symbols such as these may appear occasionally:

Some programs offer bullets in the shape of musical instruments, animals, and other objects. Sticking to simple, traditional bullets is generally more effective.

business, name of Capitalize the names of businesses and similar organizations (see CAPITALIZATION). Also capitalize shortened forms of the name.

> General Foods International, General Foods
> the Corporation for Public Broadcasting, CPB

Don't capitalize generic terms such as *corporation* or *university* when they are not preceded by a PROPER NOUN.

See also
BRAND NAME

New Names

Some companies have names that contradict these rules. Follow the company's style if the company has capital letters in the middle of its name or begins its name with a lowercase letter. Adjust your SENTENCE structure to avoid beginning a sentence with a lowercase letter.

In the 1950s
id Software would have existed only in science fiction in the 1950s.

City University of New York, *but* the university

Note that ARTICLES, short PREPOSITIONS, and CONJUNCTIONS are not capitalized within the company name.

business letter *See* LETTER, BUSINESS

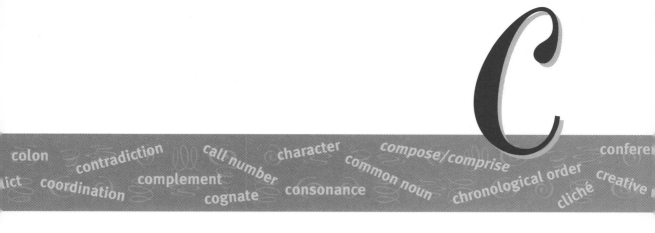

ca. The ABBREVIATION for *circa,* derived from the LATIN word meaning "around." *Ca.* means "approximately." A writer may insert *ca.* before a historical date to indicate that the exact year of an event is unknown or uncertain but can be approximated. Sometimes the abbreviation *c.* is used. Do not italicize (see ITALICS) or underline either abbreviation.

The Tempest (ca. 1611) was Shakespeare's last play.

Caldecott Medal Given by the American Library Association to the "artist of the most distinguished American Picture Book for Children published in the United States during the preceding year." The award is named in honor of the nineteenth-century English illustrator Randolph J. Caldecott.

The distinctive Caldecott bronze medal is reproduced on the dust covers of all books receiving the award. Some of the recent Caldecott winners include *Snowflake Bentley* (1999), illustrated by Mary Azarian; *Rapunzel* (1998), retold and illustrated by Paul O. Zelinsky; *Golem* (1997), written and illustrated by David Wisniewski; *Officer Buckle and Gloria* (1996), written and illustrated by Peggy Rathman; and *Smoky Night* (1995), illustrated by David Diaz.

See also
NEWBERY MEDAL
NOBEL PRIZE
PULITZER PRIZE

Net Source

For covers and reviews of recent Caldecott winners, see <http:///www.ala.org/alsc/caldecott.html>.

call number The combination of letters or numbers assigned to a book in a LIBRARY to indicate where the book is shelved. Most libraries use the call numbers assigned under one of two systems: either the DEWEY DECIMAL SYSTEM or the LIBRARY OF CONGRESS CLASSIFICATION. Both systems assign books to categories. Under the Dewey Decimal System, for example, any book about literature (other than novels) has a call number between 800 and 899, while under the Library of Congress Classification the same book has a call number beginning with the letter *P*.

See also
CATALOG, LIBRARY

can/may Use *can* to express ability; use *may* to express permission.

> You <u>can</u> play the violin very well.
> You <u>may</u> play the violin when your sister is not napping.

May also expresses possibility.

> We <u>may</u> go to the theater this weekend.

See also
AUXILIARY VERB
HELPING VERB
MODAL

cannon/canon *Cannon* refers to a large, wheeled gun. *Canon* refers to a section of prayers in some Christian churches, a particular rank of clergy, or a list of works belonging to a certain class.

Memory Jogger

Only a ca**nn**on is fully loaded (with *n*'s).

---

can't hardly, can't scarcely Nonstandard phrases. Use *can hardly* or *can scarcely* instead.

> can hardly
> I ~~can't hardly~~ wait for summer vacation.

See also
DOUBLE NEGATIVE

canto Part of a long poem. *Canto* originally came from a LATIN word meaning "song" and referred to a section of a narrative poem (see NARRATIVE POETRY) short enough to be sung by a minstrel, or poet-musician, in one singing. Later, poets sometimes called sections of their poems *cantos* to suggest their songlike qualities.

canvas/canvass *Canvas* is a heavy cloth often used for tents and bags. Artists paint on canvas. *Canvass* means "to take a POLL or SURVEY throughout an area or among certain people."

> The people with the <u>canvas</u> backpacks have come to <u>canvass</u> our neighborhood for the national census.

— Helpful Hint —

Same Pronunciation
Pronounce both *canvas* and *canvass* with the ACCENT on the first SYLLABLE.

capital/capitol The *capital* is the city that contains the seat of government of a state or country. A *capitol* is the building in which members of the government meet. Normally lowercased, *capitol* should be capitalized when it refers to the building where the U.S. House of Representatives and Senate meet. (*Capital* also refers to uppercase letters.)

Memory Jogger

The capit**ol** has a d**o**me.

capitalization *See p. 20*

card catalog *See* CATALOG, LIBRARY

cardinal number A number used for counting and to express quantity: *1, 2, 3, 4,* and so forth, whether written as a numeral or as a word. An ORDINAL NUMBER, on the other hand, expresses order: *first, second,* and so forth.

See also

NUMBER

caret The SYMBOL ^, found above the numeral *6* on a typewriter or computer keyboard. Word-processing pro-
(continues on p. 25)

CAPITALIZATION The system of beginning certain words with an uppercase, or capital, letter.

Capitalization in Sentences

Begin each SENTENCE with a capital letter. When a sentence contains another sentence in PARENTHESES, lowercase the first letter of the parenthetical sentence. When a parenthetical sentence occurs outside any other sentence, capitalize its first word. Capitalizing the first word of an INDEPENDENT CLAUSE after a COLON is optional. Follow your teacher's preference on this point.

> When David learned to read (he was only three), he liked to chant this rhyme: Read to be freed; read with speed. (He drove everyone crazy.)

Capitalization of Quotations

Direct QUOTATIONS begin with a capital letter when accompanied by a **tag** such as *he said*. If the tag interrupts a quoted sentence, do not capitalize the part of the quotation after the tag.

> Sarah asked, "What time shall we leave?"
> "Oh," her mom answered, "five o'clock is early enough."

When quoting just a word, PHRASE, or CLAUSE, capitalize or lowercase the quotation as you would if the words were not in quotation marks.

> Nick said the movie was "just great."

In traditional POETRY each line begins with a capital letter. Some modern poets do not use this style; when quoting them, follow their capitalization style.

Capitalization of Proper Nouns

Capitalize the names of specific persons, groups, places, units of time, things, and titles of works.

Personal Names

Capitalize the first, last, and middle names of people:

> Mary Elizabeth Mahoney

Also capitalize nicknames and family names when used in place of the given name. Do not capitalize these names when they are not used in place of the given name.

> After dinner Mom told me to help Buddy with
>   his homework.
> My mom thinks the new baby will be a little buddy
>   for me.

Lowercase a short PREPOSITION or an ARTICLE in a proper name.

> Mary Queen of Scots
> Louise the Larger

Some name parts such as *von, van, vander, de,* and *l'* may be capitalized or not. Follow the preference of the bearer of the name.

> Mies van der Rohe
> Mark Van Doren

Capitalize people's TITLES when they appear before their names as part of the name:

> Dr. Jan Steinmetz
> President Ewan Kohl
> Queen Elizabeth II

Ordinarily, do not capitalize titles when they are not part of the person's name.

> Jan Steinmetz, my family's <u>doctor</u>
> Ewan Kohl, the <u>president</u> of the bank
> the <u>queen</u> of England

Names of Organizations or Groups

Capitalize the names of BUSINESSES (see BUSINESS, NAME OF), government bodies, associations, nationalities or regional residents, and races. (Check with your teacher about descriptive race terms such as "white"; preferences vary.)

> <u>M</u>eredith <u>C</u>orporation
> the <u>U</u>nited <u>S</u>tates <u>S</u>enate
> the <u>M</u>ellon <u>F</u>oundation
> <u>D</u>epartment of <u>H</u>uman <u>S</u>ervices
> <u>P</u>arent-<u>T</u>eacher <u>A</u>ssociation
> the <u>I</u>rish
> <u>W</u>esterners
> our <u>J</u>ewish neighbors

Place Names

Capitalize the main words in proper names of places.

> GEOGRAPHICAL FEATURES: the <u>R</u>ed <u>R</u>iver, the <u>G</u>rand <u>C</u>anyon, the <u>G</u>reen <u>M</u>ountains, the <u>A</u>tlantic <u>O</u>cean
> NEIGHBORHOODS, CITIES, STATES, REGIONS, COUNTRIES, AND CONTINENTS: <u>L</u>ittle <u>I</u>taly, <u>S</u>an <u>F</u>rancisco, <u>N</u>evada, <u>N</u>ew <u>E</u>ngland, <u>C</u>anada, <u>A</u>ntarctica
> BUILDINGS AND STRUCTURES: the <u>F</u>ord <u>T</u>heater, the <u>S</u>tatue of <u>L</u>iberty
> ADDRESSES: 1234 <u>F</u>ifty-sixth <u>S</u>treet

PLANETS, STARS, GALAXIES, CONSTELLATIONS: the planet Jupiter, Alpha Centauri, the Milky Way, the Big Dipper

DIRECTIONAL WORDS TO REFER TO REGIONS: the Deep South, the Midwest

Do not capitalize place name words when they are used generically.

Travel north three blocks to the theater by the river.

Names of Units of Time

Capitalize proper names of historical or geological periods of time, holidays, days of the week, months, and historical events.

the Middle Ages	Saturday
the Precambrian Era	February
Ramadan	the Battle of the Bulge

Lowercase COMMON NOUNS that refer to periods of time.

the nineteenth century
yesterday
summer

Names of Things

Capitalize the proper names of things.

BRAND NAMES: Advil, Chevrolet, the Concorde (but ibuprofen, car, jet)

LANGUAGES: English, Swahili, Urdu, Old Norse

COURSE NAMES: History 101 (but my history class)

AWARDS: the Nobel Prize for Peace, an Oscar (but a blue ribbon for the hundred-yard freestyle)

Abbreviations of Proper Nouns

Capitalize an ABBREVIATION or ACRONYM for a name that is capitalized when spelled out.

> NPR (National Public Radio)
> NAFTA (North American Free Trade Agreement)

Capitalization in Titles of Works

In the TITLES of your ESSAYS and other writings and in written and artistic works you name, capitalize the first word and the last word and all other important words— not coordinate CONJUNCTIONS, ARTICLES, and PREPOSITIONS. Treat SUBTITLES like titles.

> *Harriet the Spy*
> *American History: An Introduction for Immigrants*

Special Cases of Capitalization

Besides capitalization rules for sentences, PROPER NOUNS, and titles, note the following special situations that call for capitalization.

- the FIRST-PERSON SINGULAR PRONOUN in the NOMINATIVE CASE: I
- in titles all parts of a hyphenated word, except for words such as prepositions that would not be capitalized if they stood alone in the title. (Check with your teacher about capitalizing the second part of compound numbers; preferences vary.)

> Up-to-Date Voter Regulations for In-the-Know Citizens

- the word *O,* especially in poetry (*but* oh)

Helpful Hint

Exceptions

In certain contexts your AUDIENCE may expect initial capital letters for words that the general public treats as common nouns. When writing about an organization at school, for example, you may refer to the President or Secretary. Similarly, in internal MEMOS within a business, writers may refer to the Company or the Chairman.

(continued from p. 19)

grams often include the caret among symbols you can insert from a menu of symbols. When PROOFREADING, use a caret to indicate where you want to insert something.

Jonathan hasn't his paycheck.
received
^

┌─ Helpful Hint ─☞

Beware Homonyms
Don't confuse *caret* with *carrot,* the vegetable, or *carat,* the unit of measurement.

└──────────────────┘

---

caricature Descriptive writing (see DESCRIPTION) that exaggerates certain characteristics of an individual in order to produce a ridiculous or grotesque effect and poke fun. The novelist Charles Dickens's minor CHARACTERS are often caricatures, created to underscore a social commentary or suggest lessons about certain unpleasant behavioral traits.

The term *caricature* is commonly associated with drawings or cartoons, particularly political cartoons. Editorial pages from a city newspaper typically feature graphic caricatures of national politicians with their noticeable physical features highlighted and exaggerated. Caricature was particularly popular during the eighteenth century. In France the artist Honoré Daumier published numerous caricatures of French politicians.

See also
HUMOR
PARODY
SATIRE

case *See p. 26*

case study A problem-centered writing situation in which you are provided with a themed collection of ESSAYS or topically organized information so that you can focus on your writing instead of gathering information. Your task is to examine the information provided and use it to present a written solution to a problem. The document-based question on the ADVANCED PLACEMENT examination in American history is an example of the case-study approach.

(continues on p. 29)

CASE The form of a NOUN or PRONOUN that indicates a word's grammatical function in a SENTENCE. MODERN ENGLISH has three cases, but for nouns two of the cases have the same form.

> NOMINATIVE CASE: The <u>book</u> is a <u>novel</u>.
> OBJECTIVE CASE: Put the <u>book</u> on the <u>table</u>.
> POSSESSIVE CASE: Who is the <u>book's</u> author?

In the first example one underlined noun is the SUBJECT of the sentence, and one is the PREDICATE NOMINATIVE. In the second example the first underlined noun is a DIRECT OBJECT, and the second underlined noun is the OBJECT OF A PREPOSITION. In the third example the underlined noun is modifying another noun. Notice that the NOMINATIVE CASE—sometimes called the **subjective case**—of a noun and the OBJECTIVE CASE take the same form.

The matter of case is more complex for personal pronouns. Use the nominative, or subjective, case when the pronoun is a subject or predicate nominative:

> <u>I</u> like peaches.
> It is <u>I</u>.

Use the objective case when the pronoun is a direct object, INDIRECT OBJECT, or object of a preposition.

> My parents love <u>me</u>.
> My brother gave <u>me</u> a present.
> The present was for <u>me</u>.

The POSSESSIVE CASE (sometimes called the genitive case) comes in two forms for some pronouns. Use one kind of possessive pronoun as a MODIFIER before a noun. Use the other possessive pronoun after a form of *be*.

That is <u>my</u> present.

That present is <u>mine</u>.

Here is a list of pronoun case forms.

Nominative (Subjective)	Objective	Possessive (Before a Noun)	Possessive (After a Form of *Be*)
I	me	my	mine
we	us	our	ours
he	him	his	his
she	her	her	hers
you	you	your	yours
they	them	their	theirs
who	whom	whose	whose
whoever	whomever		

It is I vs. *It is me*

Pronoun cases can sometimes cause problems. One such problem occurs when the pronoun is the predicate nominative after a LINKING VERB. In FORMAL situations many teachers prefer the nominative case: "It is I"; in INFORMAL speech and writing, teachers may allow "It is me."

Who vs. *Whom*

Similarly, formal situations demand the use of the objective pronouns *whom* and *whomever* when the pronoun is a direct object, an indirect object, or an object of a preposition.

> <u>Whom</u> did you ask?
> To <u>whom</u> did you give the present?
> Give a present to <u>whomever</u> you wish.

In casual speech and writing, however, *whom* and *whomever* can sound stuffy. For this reason "Who did you ask?" "Who did you give the present to?" and "Give a present to whoever you wish" are common in these situations.

Pronouns in Compound Structures

A third problem involves deciding which case to use when one part of a compound structure (such as a COM-POUND SUBJECT) is a pronoun. In a sentence such as "Me and Roger went rowing," you can catch the error and correct it by trying the pronoun alone. Since you would never say "Me went rowing," you know that the correct pronoun is *I*.

> Roger and <u>I</u> went rowing.

The same principle applies in the objective case. Since you would never say "Kathy went rowing with I," you know that the correct pronoun when the object of the preposition is compound is *me*.

> Kathy went rowing with Roger and <u>me</u>.

— Helpful Hint — 👉

Who or Whom?

To decide whether *who* or *whom* is correct, try substituting the word *he* or *him* in the relevant part of the sentence. If *he* sounds right, use *who;* if *him* sounds right, use *whom.*

> The police asked us <u>who/whom</u> we had seen entering the building.

Whom is correct because it sounds right to say "We had seen <u>him</u> entering the building."

(continued from p. 25)

Some textbooks use the term *case study* to refer to a detailed examination of one instance so that the reader can generalize from that model and learn about the larger class or phenomenon. For example, in teaching students how to write strong DESCRIPTIONS, a textbook might offer a case study about a person whose job calls for writing descriptions to accompany museum exhibits.

cast The actors and actresses in a dramatic production. For many years and in many cultures, women were forbidden by law to be onstage. During Shakespeare's day all female parts were played by males—often by young boys whose voices had not yet changed.

See also
DRAMATIS PERSONAE

catalog, library A list of the contents of a LIBRARY, arranged according to a system that allows users to find books and other materials on the library's shelves.

Card catalogs, designed before there were COMPUTERS, consist of deep, narrow drawers that contain alphabetically arranged cards for every item in the library: books, tapes, records, pamphlets, and the like (see ALPHABETICAL ORDER). A CALL NUMBER, usually printed on the upper left-hand corner of the card, is the same call number written on the spine of the book and enables the user to find the item on the library's shelves.

AUTHOR cards are filed alphabetically according to the author's last name. Thus, a book by Thomas Hardy would be filed under *Hardy, Thomas.* Title cards are arranged according to the first word in the item's title (excluding *a, an,* and *the).* Thus, Hardy's book *The Return of the Native* would be filed under *Return of the Native, The.* Subject cards are filed according to topic, so

See also
DEWEY DECIMAL SYSTEM
LIBRARY OF CONGRESS
CLASSIFICATION

a user looking for information about the beliefs of different religions throughout the world would look in the card catalog under *Religion.* Cross-reference cards tell the library user that items about a particular topic are filed under another heading. Thus, if you looked under the heading *Conservation of Wildlife,* a cross-reference card might point you to the place in the card catalog where the titles of books on this topic can be found: *Wildlife conservation.*

All cards (other than cross-reference cards) provide complete bibliographic information about the item, including the author's full name, the complete title of the book (including any SUBTITLES), the publisher, the date of publication, the book's length, and information regarding illustrations.

Although a number of libraries continue to rely on paper card catalogs, many others have computerized their catalogs. Some make both systems available, and in some libraries older items are cataloged in paper files, while new items are listed on the computer.

Computer catalogs function in much the same way paper catalogs do. If the user enters an author's name, all the library's books by that author appear. If a title is entered, the "card" for that title appears. If a subject is entered, "cards" for all books about that subject appear (often requiring the user to narrow the topic).

For library users computerized catalogs have at least four advantages: (1) They tell the user if a book is checked out or is still on the shelf; (2) they allow the user to reserve a checked-out book; (3) they usually indicate whether or not a book that the library does not have is available elsewhere, perhaps at another branch in a countywide library system; and (4) they are accessible from remote locations, such as home computers.

catharsis A term used by the ancient Greek philosopher Aristotle in his *Poetics* to describe the effect of dramatic TRAGEDY on an AUDIENCE. The term comes from the Greek word *katharsis,* meaning "purging" or "purification." Aristotle believed that tragedy aroused "terror and pity" in the audience and, in so doing, caused the catharsis, or release, of those emotions.

Some people believe tragedy presents a moral lesson to the audience. They argue that the fear and pity the audience feels in response to the HERO's fall provide a warning not to tempt fate in a similar fashion. Others believe that when the audience experiences fear vicariously through art, it identifies with the tragic PROTAGONIST, universalizing his or her experience. As a result, they argue, tragedy has a psychologically healthy effect on the viewer or reader. The final scene of Shakespeare's *Romeo and Juliet,* for example, leads the audience through horror and grief as first Romeo and then Juliet kill themselves.

cause and effect *See* DEVELOPMENT, METHODS OF; ESSAY

cede, ceed, sede Almost all English words ending with the sound "seed" are spelled *cede.* For example:

> intercede, recede, precede

The following are the only exceptions.

> supersede
> exceed, proceed, succeed

See also
SPELLING

cedilla A DIACRITICAL MARK placed under a letter to indicate a change in the usual pronunciation of the letter. The cedilla is used in several languages, including PORTUGUESE, ROMANIAN, and Turkish. English readers, however, are

See also
ACCENT (DIACRITICAL MARK)
CIRCUMFLEX
DIERESIS
TILDE

most likely to encounter it in words borrowed from FRENCH, such as *façade.* Here the cedilla indicates that the *c* is pronounced as an *s* rather than as a *k.*

See also

ASIAN LANGUAGES, INFLUENCE ON ENGLISH

FRENCH, INFLUENCE ON ENGLISH

LATIN, INFLUENCE ON ENGLISH

and other languages

Celtic languages, influence on English A group of European languages spoken by the Celts, a cultural and linguistic group that once extended across much of the European continent and the British Isles.

The Celtic languages include two groups. The British (or Britannic) Celtic languages include Welsh and Breton (which are still spoken) and Cornish, Cumbric, and Pictish (which are extinct). The Irish Celtic languages include Irish and Scottish Gaelic, which are still spoken in Ireland, the Isle of Man, Scotland, and Wales. Common MODERN ENGLISH words borrowed from British Celtic include *glen* and *crag.*

central idea *See* MAIN IDEA; THESIS STATEMENT; TOPIC SENTENCE

cf. ABBREVIATION of the LATIN word for "confer" (meaning "compare"). *Cf.* appears chiefly in the **footnotes, end notes,** or BIBLIOGRAPHY of scholarly works. It draws the reader's attention to similarities and differences. Do not use *cf.* in the **body** of an ESSAY; instead, spell out the word *compare.*

See also

CHARACTERIZATION, METHODS OF

character An imaginary person—or an animal or thing presented as a person—appearing in a fictional NARRATIVE or dramatic work (see DRAMA); also a person in NONFICTION. Characters are usually thought of as FLAT or ROUND, STATIC or DYNAMIC.

A flat character is one-dimensional; he or she presents a single personality trait or behavior. Extreme focus on one dominant trait to the exclusion of others creates a CARICATURE. Charles Dickens's Uriah Heep is one such flat character.

Novelist E. M. Forster (1879–1970) introduced the term *round* to describe those characters who are so complex and fully developed that they become alive, allowing readers to live their joys and sorrows with them. Jess Aarons in Paterson's *Bridge to Terabithia,* Billie Jo in Hesse's *Out of the Dust,* and Shakespeare's Hamlet are all round characters. Their sensitivities to their predicaments give them humanity.

A static character changes little, if at all, in the course of a narrative, no matter what events he or she confronts. A dynamic character, on the other hand, is changed by experience. Nora's slamming of the door at the end of Ibsen's *A Doll's House* is a clear indication that Nora is no longer the twittering "little skylark" of the beginning of the play. In Twain's *The Adventures of Huckleberry Finn* Huck's recognition that it would be wrong for him to betray Jim—no matter what society believes—demonstrates his moral maturation.

characterization, methods of The ways in which writers describe or show us their CHARACTERS. In DIRECT CHARACTERIZATION a writer uses EXPOSITION to tell the reader about a character. For example, Jane Austen (1775–1817) offers this information about her title character:

Model

> Emma Woodhouse, handsome, clever, and rich, with a comfortable home and happy disposition…had lived nearly twenty-one years in the world with very little to distress or vex her…. The real evils indeed of

See also
SHOWING VS. TELLING

> [Emma's] situation were the power of having rather too much her own way, and a disposition to think a little too well of herself....

Little is left to imagination as Austen draws her character.

Other writers commonly use INDIRECT CHARACTERIZATION. Here actions, speech, thoughts, physical appearance, and comments by others show us characters and help us understand their MOTIVATIONS. In Mark Twain's *The Adventures of Tom Sawyer* watching Tom persuade his friends to help him whitewash a fence convinces readers that Tom is imaginative and willing to spend a great deal of energy avoiding unpleasant tasks.

Active readers (see ACTIVE READING) often analyze characters. One strategy is to search a text for passages that focus on the character. Look for passages that offer physical description, typical actions, things the character says that seem particularly significant, or comments others make about him or her. Try to collect samples from the beginning, middle, and end of the text to help you identify character changes. As you review your collection of passages, use the evidence to help you make several statements about the character's personality (for example, "Tom is persuasive" and "Tom doesn't like boring jobs" are two statements you might make after reading about the whitewashing incident).

When writing, you often need to present DESCRIPTIONS of people. If you are writing NONFICTION, try BRAINSTORMING a list of DETAILS. What does this individual do and say? How does he or she dress? How does he or she gesture while talking? What is important to him or her? What setting might be typical? Then review your list to determine a dominant impression. Try to find one or two words that characterize the individual. Then select the details from your list that most clearly present that impression.

Writing FICTION requires the same process, although it is more complex because you have to rely on your imagination. You may find it helpful to create a character chart.

Character Chart

Character Name:							
Actions	Thoughts/ Motivation	Statements	Appearance	Statements by Others about Character	Reactions of Others to Character	Thoughts of Others about Character	

Use the chart to help you plan how to show your readers your character and his or her situation.

character sketch Descriptive writing that provides readers with a picture of a CHARACTER, whether fictional or real. While it is important to give readers a rich physical DESCRIPTION, a good character sketch conveys the subject's personality as well. It answers such questions as "What kind of person is this?" "What is important to him or her?" "How do others react to him or her?"

Here is a sample character sketch. As you read it, notice how action reveals character.

Model

Horace raised his left forefinger in the direction of the waitress. "Check, please," he called.

When the rectangular plastic tray arrived, Horace carefully lifted the itemized accounting and smoothed it on the table for inspection. Hamburger, $2.95 (a dollar cheaper than a cheeseburger, he thought with satisfaction), small fries (lots of ketchup adds bulk), and an iced tea (the refills are free). The total said $4.75. Horace frowned and went over the numbers a second time.

As the waitress passed the table again, Horace signaled for her attention. "Here, I think you've made a mistake," he told her. "You've added incorrectly. The total should be $4.65, not $4.75." He paused for effect. "You've overcharged me by a dime."

While the waitress took the check back for correction, Horace reached into his back pocket for his wallet. Removing four singles, he held them in his left hand while searching his right pocket for change, counting out two quarters, a dime, and five pennies.

When the waitress returned with the corrected bill, he tucked the money on her tray and waved her off with a grand gesture.

I like eating out now and then, he thought. He ate the last piece of parsley from his plate and dug the lemon from the bottom of his glass. Standing, he reached into his pocket for the tip. Reluctantly, he slipped a quarter under the edge of the plate and left the café sucking on his lemon. Yup, he thought. I like eating out. Especially on my birthday.

When writing a character sketch, begin by collecting physical DETAILS. If you are writing about a real person, observe him or her closely, jotting down as much information as you can. Answer questions such as the following:

- How does she hold her hands when talking?
- What do others do when he comes into the room?
- Where is she typically seen? Doing what?

If you are writing FICTION, begin by picturing your character as completely as possible.

- What is his or her name?
- Where does your character live?
- Do you know anybody on whom you can model your invented character? (If you do, observe the real person's traits to help you in describing your fictional character.)
- What is important to your character?

The more precisely you can identify your character, the easier it will be for you to write a character sketch that will really make him or her come alive for readers.

After you have collected your information, look it over asking yourself, "What is the dominant impression I want to convey with my character sketch? What do I want my readers to understand about this person?" Choose those details that present that impression most clearly.

Keep in mind that the same details might be used to convey different impressions, depending on your DICTION. For example, perhaps you want to describe your character's bright eyes. You might describe them as twinkling (revealing a sense of humor), or sparkling (showing excitement and energy), or flashing (indicating anger), or glistening (suggesting the possibility of tears).

After you finish your piece, read it to friends or family members and ask them to tell you what they think of the person you are describing. If what they tell you matches the impression you intended to convey, your character sketch is successful.

See also

BAR GRAPH

FLOW CHART

chart A presentation in a visual form such as a diagram, GRAPH, TABLE, time line, or other figure. Some teachers and books use the term **graphic organizer** instead of *chart*. Charts take different visual forms—from the circular PIE CHART and VENN DIAGRAM to the gridlike LINE GRAPH and COMPARISON FRAME.

Writers and speakers include charts in a piece of writing and in an ORAL PRESENTATION to help their AUDIENCE take in and understand complex information. An effective chart presents the information more succinctly and vividly than words could do alone. Often, a chart communicates clearly because it helps the audience see the *relationship* between pieces of data—for example, not only how much money each class contributed to a fund-raising effort but also how well each class did compared with the others.

As clear as charts are supposed to be, they cannot simply be dropped into writing or speeches. You have to prepare your audience for them—and help your audience interpret them—by writing or saying something such as the following:

> The next chart, Figure 1, shows contributions by each class to the fund-raising project. Clearly, the combined eighth-grade classes led the school.

Many software packages—word-processing packages as well as spreadsheet and presentation packages—can help you with the work of creating your own charts.

— Helpful Hint —

Heads for Charts
Number the charts in your work consecutively, and give each one a title, as in the examples that accompany this entry.

Working with charts as with text, if you copy a figure from another source or even if you use only data from another source (putting it into an original chart), you must credit the source (see DOCUMENTATION).

Figure 1. Contributions by Class

Grade	Homeroom	Amount Donated	Total by Grade
6	201	$15.30	$63.55
	202	$12.75	
	203	$19.00	
	204	$16.50	
7	205	$14.00	$45.25
	206	$14.25	
	207	$17.00	
8	208	$22.00	$75.50
	209	$30.00	
	210	$23.50	

Figure 2. Changing Music-Delivery Systems for Baby-Boom Generation

1950s	1960s	1970s	1980s	1990s+
vinyl 45	portable radio	"Walkman" (radio & cassette)	CD	CD-ROM
	transistor radio	"stereo"	MTV	computer download
	"hi-fi"			

Figure 3. Evolution of Germanic Languages

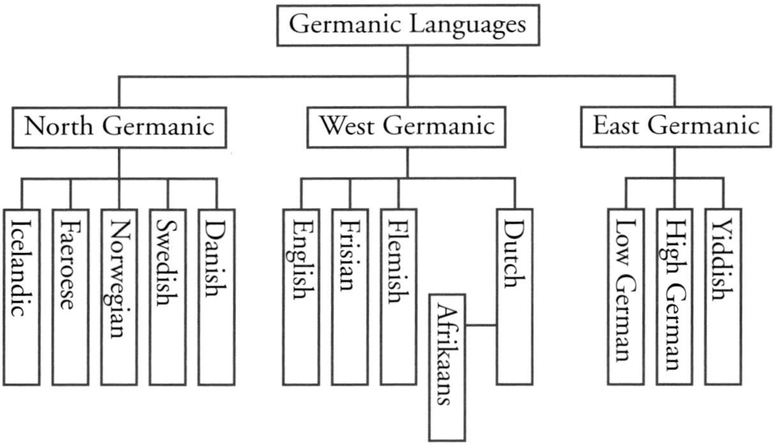

```
                        Germanic Languages
        ┌───────────────────────┼───────────────────────┐
   North Germanic          West Germanic           East Germanic
  ┌──┬──┬──┬──┬──┐      ┌──┬──┬──┬────┬──┐       ┌──┬──┬──┐
Icelandic Faeroese Norwegian Swedish Danish  English Frisian Flemish Afrikaans Dutch  Low German High German Yiddish
```

See also
┌ ─ ─ ─
┊ SENTENCE COMBINING

choppy sentences, fixing Combining a series of short SEN-TENCES to improve the clarity and flow of the ideas they express.

> CHOPPY: The costumes for the play have arrived.
> I will pick my costume up this weekend.
> Mine is a frog costume.
>
> IMPROVED: The costumes for the play have arrived, and I will pick up my frog costume this weekend.

Sometimes one sentence contains an idea that is more important than the ideas in the sentences around it. In that case you may need to subordinate the minor ideas (see SUBORDINATION).

> CHOPPY: The students asked the teacher to postpone the test.
> The teacher became very angry.
>
> IMPROVED: When the students asked the teacher to postpone the test, he became very angry.

Short sentences call attention to themselves. Use them carefully for EMPHASIS, one at a time.

> Many people in this town think football is the only sport worth spending time and money on. They are quite mistaken!

choral reading Dramatic ORAL PRESENTATION of a piece of literature. In a choral reading presenters may take turns reading separately and together. Unlike plays, choral readings do not call for presenters to move around on stage; ordinarily presenters stand still or sit, often on stools.

See also
READERS' THEATER

chorus (in drama) Originally, in the plays of ancient Greece, a group of singers and dancers who commented on the DRAMA's action without taking part in it. At first the chorus provided moral or social commentary, expressing the views of the general populace in response to the play's action. As drama developed, however, the chorus became less and less important, often being relegated to nothing more than an entertaining filler between acts.

Essentially a committee, the chorus held views that were often conservative and therefore at odds with the views or actions of the main CHARACTERS. In contemporary drama a single character will often step into the role of the chorus and express the views held by the community as a whole.

chorus (in song) A REFRAIN, or regularly repeated line or VERSE. The chorus is a common feature of American folk music, particularly in the form known as a BALLAD, in which it provides an opportunity for the AUDIENCE to join a soloist who sings the VERSES that advance the NARRATIVE line.

See also
COHERENCE
IMPORTANCE, ORDER OF
LOGICAL ORDER
SPATIAL ORDER
TRANSITION

chronological order One way writers organize information to make it easy for readers to understand; also called **time order.** When writing DIRECTIONS, be careful to present each step in the order in which it should be done. When preparing to write a NARRATIVE, make a quick list of the events in the order in which they happened.

If each event builds on the last with increasing excitement, you may wish to tell your story in straight chronological order, beginning with the first event and presenting each subsequent event in sequence. Sometimes writers capture their reader's attention by using a technique called FLASHBACK. Beginning with a moment near the end of the tale, they weave necessary background information into the developing story line. When the conclusion of a story isn't as important as the events that lead up to it, a writer might choose to use a technique called FLASH FORWARD, presenting the conclusion first, then returning to the beginning and telling the rest of the story in chronological sequence.

circle graph *See* PIE CHART

circular reasoning *See* BEGGING THE QUESTION

See also
DIACRITICAL MARK

circumflex SYMBOL ^ placed over a VOWEL to indicate something about its pronunciation. Some languages have letters that incorporate the circumflex. An English-language DICTIONARY may use a circumflex to show how to pronounce a vowel sound.

air (âr)

circumlocution Roundabout, often redundant expression (see REDUNDANCY). Circumlocutions create a bulky STYLE because they use many words instead of one or two. Once you learn to identify and eliminate circumlocutions, your PROSE will become tighter and more effective.

See also
WORDINESS

BULKY: At this point in time we are in possession of important information to check into.

IMPROVED: Now we have important information to check.

Here are some common circumlocutions and possible substitutes.

along the lines of	like
as to whether	whether
at about	about
at all times	always
at the present time	now
complete monopoly	monopoly
continue on	continue
cooperate together	cooperate
customary practice	practice
due to the fact that	because
during the course of	during
each and every	every
in many cases	often

in order to	to
in regard to	about
in the event that	if
past experience	experience
personal friend	friend
provided that	if

citation *See* BIBLIOGRAPHY; DOCUMENTATION; MODERN LAN-GUAGE ASSOCIATION; WORKS-CITED LIST

cite/sight/site *Cite* means "to refer to" or "to mention."

Be sure to <u>cite</u> your sources in the bibliography.

Sight, as either a NOUN or a VERB, refers to vision.

We caught <u>sight</u> of our friends at the picnic.

Site refers to a specific location.

The new store's <u>site</u> allows for plenty of parking.

See also

ACCURACY, IN WRITING
AWKWARD WRITING
COHERENCE
IMPORTANCE, ORDER OF
LOGICAL ORDER
REVISING

clarity, in writing The orderly presentation of complete information and ideas so as not to confuse a reader. Effective writers choose the organizational mode that best suits their content, their AUDIENCE, and their PURPOSE. For example, when writing a NARRATIVE, an effective writer uses CHRONOLOGICAL ORDER. When writing DESCRIPTION, he or she uses SPATIAL ORDER.

Sometimes writing is unclear because the AUTHOR has left out information that a reader needs for understanding. When you are ready to check your piece for clarity, reread it, asking yourself "What else does my reader need to know?" and "Does this information connect with what I said before?" "Does it connect with what I say next?"

Sometimes a sentence is unclear because it is a SENTENCE FRAGMENT. To remedy this problem, look at each sentence in turn and identify its VERB. Once you have located the verb, find its SUBJECT by asking yourself, "Who or what (verb)?" If you are missing the verb or cannot find its subject, you have a fragment and need to revise.

classicism A term referring to the art produced in ancient Greece and Rome, or to art inspired by the art of ancient Greece and Rome. Ancient Greece and Rome valued harmony, restraint, and idealism in art, characteristics that have been imitated by artists during other periods of classicism.

Periods of classicism in the visual arts, literature, and music generally overlap. During the eighteenth century, for example, Thomas Jefferson was influenced by the style and principles of ancient Doric architecture as he designed his famous home at Monticello in Virginia. During the same period the work of such writers as the British poet Alexander Pope and the French philosopher Voltaire embodied classicism's emphasis on form and order.

See also
NEOCLASSICISM
ROMANTICISM

classification and division, as methods of development

Two ways of organizing information in EXPOSITION, writing that explains.

When you look at a number or group of items and separate those items into subgroups on the basis of a particular characteristic, you are classifying. For example, you can classify the animals in a zoo as land animals, water animals, and animals that live both on land and in water. Your primary purpose is to group, or classify, the animals into categories according to their habitats.

However, when you examine any one specific animal and break it down into its constituent parts (its individual organs, limbs, head and tail, for example) and then discuss each part separately, you are engaged in a different process: division.

clause *See p. 48*

clause *See p. 48*

See also
TRITENESS

cliché An overused expression, often a SIMILE that has been repeated so often that it has lost its effectiveness. A cliché pretends to offer a vivid way of seeing something, but it fails because its phrasing is so commonplace that readers no longer visualize the picture offered. Clichés include

> mad as a hornet
> Don't rock the boat.
> window of opportunity
> ladder of success
> sly as a fox
> between a rock and a hard place
> over the hill
> tip of the iceberg
> back yourself into a corner
> plant your roots

Avoid clichés in your writing. Be particularly on the lookout for them at the EDITING stage of the WRITING PROCESS. One way to notice clichés in your writing is to read your work aloud. Reexamine anything that sounds too familiar.

climactic sentence *See* PERIODIC SENTENCE

climax That part of a NARRATIVE at which the CONFLICT reaches its highest point because of a decisive action or decision. In DRAMA the climax is often thought of as the **turning point** of the action.

See also
DÉNOUEMENT
NOVEL
PLOT
RESOLUTION
SHORT STORY

conflict and complications — climax

exposition — resolution

clincher sentence The last sentence in a PARAGRAPH when used to provide readers with a SUMMARY or conclusion. The clincher sentence is often a restatement of the TOPIC SENTENCE. Because a clincher sentence conveys a sense of finality or closure on an idea, not every paragraph should have one. A clincher sentence is most effective when you wish to make a strong statement at the end of a section of your ESSAY before taking a different direction or beginning a new line of your discussion.

closing, letter Also known as the complimentary close, the graceful good-bye at the end of a LETTER. Your closing can be FORMAL or INFORMAL, personal, businesslike, or modern. As with the SALUTATION, the closing should be appropriate for the TONE of the letter and should reflect your relationship with the recipient. If your salutation is a businesslike *Dear Sir:* don't use an informal, warm closing like *All the best.*

Some sample closings include the following:

See also
HEADING, LETTER
INSIDE ADDRESS
SIGNATURE

(continues on p. 51)

See also

THAT/WHICH
THAT/WHO
WHO WHOM

CLAUSE A group of words that contains a SUBJECT and a VERB. Some clauses can stand alone as sentences.

> I ordered vanilla ice cream.

Some clauses, however, can't stand alone as sentences because, in addition to a subject and a verb, they contain something called a subordinator, which turns the group of words into a nonsentence.

Dependent and Independent Clauses

The example sentence above, "I ordered vanilla ice cream," is an example of an INDEPENDENT CLAUSE, sometimes called a **main clause.** It has a subject and a verb, and it can stand alone as a complete sentence. Sometimes two main clauses can be put together with a coordinate CONJUNCTION preceded by a COMMA.

> INDEPENDENT CLAUSE
> I ordered vanilla ice cream,
>
> INDEPENDENT CLAUSE
> but my brother ordered chocolate.

In the preceding sentence each of the underlined clauses can stand alone as a complete sentence; both are independent clauses.

A second type of clause is called a DEPENDENT CLAUSE, or sometimes a **subordinate clause.** A dependent clause has a subject and a verb but also a subordinator such as *because, if, although, that, which,* or *when.*

> INDEPENDENT CLAUSE
> I ordered vanilla ice cream
>
> DEPENDENT CLAUSE
> because I don't like chocolate.

The preceding sentence, then, has two clauses: an independent clause and a dependent clause.

Three Kinds of Dependent Clauses

Adjective Clauses

One type of dependent clause is called an ADJECTIVE CLAUSE, or RELATIVE CLAUSE. An adjective clause acts like an ADJECTIVE to modify a NOUN or a PRONOUN. It is introduced by the words *that, which, who, whom, whose, when,* or *where.*

> The glass <u>that fell to the floor</u> broke.
> The glass, <u>which belonged to my grandmother</u>, fell to the floor and broke.
> The boy <u>who bumped the glass</u> was scolded by his father.

In each of the preceding sentences, the dependent clause is an adjective clause that modifies a noun.

Adjective clauses are either RESTRICTIVE or NONRESTRICTIVE. A restrictive adjective clause provides additional information about the noun; the information is necessary to identify the noun.

> Students <u>who graduate from Washington High School</u> generally do well in college.

In the preceding example "who graduate from Washington High School" is a restrictive adjective clause. The sentence says nothing about students in general, only about a restricted group of students.

In contrast, a nonrestrictive adjective clause provides additional but unnecessary information.

> Washington High graduates, <u>who generally come from the south part of town</u>, tend to do well in college.

Punctuation Pointer

Follow an introductory adverb clause with a comma.

> <u>When the gun sounded</u>, the runners took off.

Put commas around an adverb clause that interrupts an independent clause.

> The race, <u>although it was short</u>, seemed to last forever.

In general, do not precede an adverb clause at the end of a sentence with a comma.

> They took off <u>when the gun sounded</u>.

Use commas around a nonrestrictive clause, not around a restrictive clause.

> RESTRICTIVE: The dog that bit me got away.

> NONRESTRICTIVE: The dog, which wasn't wearing a collar, got away.

The preceding sentence makes a statement about *all* Washington High graduates. The relative clause, "who generally come from the south part of town," is not necessary and could be omitted.

Adverb Clauses

A second type of dependent clause is called an ADVERB CLAUSE. Adverb clauses serve the same function as ADVERBS; that is, they modify a VERB or even a sentence as a whole.

> When the strike ends, the workers will return to their jobs.

Here, "When the strike ends" is an adverb clause; it plays the same role in the sentence that the adverb *then* would play.

> The workers will then return to their jobs.

Noun Clauses

Noun clauses, like simple NOUNS, serve as subjects or OBJECTS in sentences.

> That the book was too long was an opinion shared by many readers.

In the preceding sentence "That the book was too long" is a clause that serves as the subject of the verb *was.*

(continued from p. 47)

FORMAL: Very truly yours,
Respectfully yours,

LESS FORMAL: Sincerely,
Cordially,
Yours truly,

PERSONAL: Best wishes,   With affection,
Warmest regards, With sympathy,
Thanks,   As ever,
Love,   Your friend,

MODERN: See ya,
Cheers,
Later,

> ## Punctuation Pointer
>
> Capitalize the first letter of the closing, and follow the closing with a COMMA.

cloze paragraph A device used to test reading comprehension and language sense. A cloze (short for *closure)* paragraph replaces words in a passage with blanks that students must fill in. Technically, cloze paragraphs leave a blank for every fifth or seventh word regardless of its importance, but some cloze paragraphs have a modified format in which critical words that students should know are omitted. Students may refer to a list of possible answers at the end of the exercise (see p. 52) or (sometimes) to a list of choices beneath each blank.

Model

> What I must do is all that (1)_____ me, not what the people (2)_____. This rule, equally arduous in actual and in intellectual (3)_____, may serve for the whole distinction between greatness and (4)_____. It is the harder, because you will always

find those who think they know what is your (5)_____ better than you know it. It is easy in the world to live after the world's (6)_____; it is easy in (7)_____ to live after our own; but the great man is he who in the midst of the (8)_____ keeps with perfect sweetness the independence of solitude.

—Ralph Waldo Emerson, "Self-Reliance"

> **Word Box**
>
> | | |
> |---|---|
> | concerns | meanness |
> | crowd | opinion |
> | duty | solitude |
> | life | think |

See also

clustering A visual method of representing ideas on a specific topic.

Once you have selected a topic for writing, you may use clustering as a strategy for generating ideas during PREWRITING. Write your topic in a circle in the middle of a blank page. Then surround the first circle with words and phrases representing key ideas about your topic. Circle each key idea, and link each to your topic with straight lines. Treat each key idea as the center of a new idea cluster and radiate another level of ideas.

Your completed diagram provides you with a visual representation of your content. Study your diagram to determine (1) whether each cluster really fits the main topic; (2) whether any clusters need to be combined, divided, or expanded; and (3) in what order you want to present each cluster.

You may also use clustering as a means of organizing your thinking about a reading assignment. For example, a cluster such as the second one on the next page might help

Clustering for Prewriting

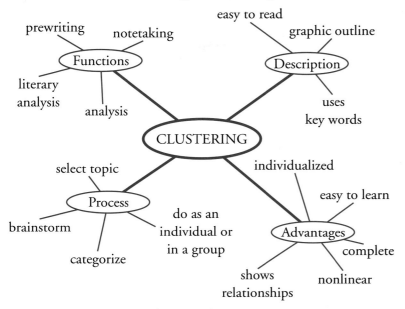

Clustering during Reading

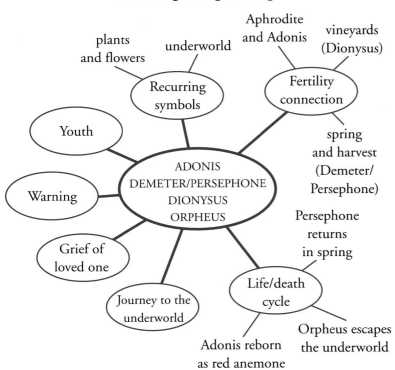

you see the similarities in the MYTHS of Adonis, Demeter and Persephone, Dionysus, and Orpheus.

coarse/course *Coarse* means "rough," "heavy," or "unrefined." The NOUN *course* means "class" or "route"; the VERB *course* means "to flow." Use *course* in the expression *of course.*

> Sand with <u>coarse</u> sandpaper at the beginning of your project; later, use fine sandpaper.
>
> What <u>course</u> do you have second period?
>
> A river may <u>course</u> through the mountains.

See also
INDO-EUROPEAN
  LANGUAGES

cognate A word that shares a ROOT with a word in another language. For example, the English word *father* and the Spanish word *padre,* which share the same meaning, are cognates, both coming from the Latin root *pater,* meaning "father."

Some cognates look and sound alike—for example, the English word *donation* and the Spanish word *donación,* which both mean "gift." Some cognates look and sound less similar—for example the English word *king* and the German word *König,* which both refer to a kind of sovereign.

— **Helpful Hint** —

Word Power
Studying a foreign language will help you understand new English words you come across.

See also
UNITY

coherence The easy-to-follow flow between SENTENCES and PARAGRAPHS; such a flow helps a reader move through a piece of writing.

Coherent writing is logical and orderly. You can achieve coherence by using effective TRANSITIONS, repeating important words or ideas, introducing a PRONOUN or a SYNONYM to refer to a previously stated NOUN, and using parallel sentence structures (see PARALLELISM). Improving coherence is a task you should attend to during the WRITING-PROCESS stage called REVISING.

The following paragraph from the Gettysburg Address illustrates how President Abraham Lincoln achieved coherence.

Model

> But, in a larger sense, we (can not) dedicate—we (can not) consecrate—we (can not) hallow—this ground. The <u>brave men</u>, living and dead, <u>who</u> struggled here, have consecrated it, far above our poor power to add or detract. The world will little note, nor long remember what we say here, but it can never forget what <u>they</u> did here. It is for us, the living, rather, to be dedicated here to the unfinished work which <u>they</u> who fought here have thus far so nobly advanced. It is rather for us to be here dedicated to the great task remaining before us—that from <u>these honored dead</u> we take increased devotion to that cause for which <u>they</u> gave the last full measure of devotion—that we here highly resolve that <u>these dead</u> shall not have died in vain—that this nation, under God, shall have a new birth of freedom—and that government <u>of the people</u>, <u>by the people</u>, <u>for the people</u>, shall not perish from the earth.

OVALS SHOW REPETITION.

SINGLE UNDER-SCORES SHOW SYNONYMS AND PRONOUNS.

RECTANGLES SHOW REPETITION AND TRANSITION.

DOUBLE UNDER-SCORES SHOW PARALLELISM.

Checklist

FOCUS ON COHERENCE

Follow this advice when REVISING.

1. Ask yourself, "Have I left out something a reader needs to know?"
2. Does your INTRODUCTION clearly signal the MAIN IDEA and prepare your reader for the information that will follow?
3. Write a one- or two-word SUMMARY in the margin. (If you can't do this, you may have too many ideas in that paragraph.)
4. Read over your marginal notes. Does the order in which you present each idea make sense?
5. Reread each paragraph. Work sentence by sentence to see if each idea connects to the previous one, as well as to the one that follows.
6. Ask several friendly readers to mark places where they had trouble following your thoughts.

coined word Also called a neologism, a word that is consciously created (as opposed to a word that enters the language through the natural processes of language development). *Laser* was formed from **l**ight **a**mplification by **s**timulated **e**mission of **r**adiation. Coined words such as *telephone, airplane, kleenex,* and *xerox* have become generally accepted, although teachers and corporations still prefer *tissue* and *copy machine* for the last two.

collaborative learning A broad term (sometimes used synonomously with *cooperative learning)* for different forms of group work including, but not limited to, peer tutoring, group classwork, and extended group projects.

Unlike **cooperative learning** participants, each of whom is given a single task (such as timekeeper, recorder, illustrator, or director), collaborative learning participants are equal in their contributions to the group effort and in their responsibilities for its success. For example, in peer tutoring, students work together to ensure that all members of the group have an equal understanding of the material. Or groups may each be given a different issue to explore when studying a novel and then asked to report their findings to the class as a whole. Working collaboratively, each student leaves class with a richer understanding.

collective noun NOUN that names a group—for example, *group, team, family, herd, committee, quartet.* Collective nouns are SINGULAR or PLURAL, depending on the meaning of the sentence as a whole. When the collective noun refers to the group as a single unit, it takes singular VERBS and PRONOUNS.

> The team <u>has</u> another game tomorrow; so far <u>its</u> record is 0 and 4.
> The herd <u>is pastured</u> in the south meadow near <u>its</u> stock pond.

Helpful Hint

Changing Subjects

Because a collective noun may sound awkward with a plural verb, good writers often revise their sentences to avoid such constructions. Consider the following revision of the fourth example.

Today the <u>members</u> of the quartet get <u>their</u> paychecks.

When the collective noun refers to the multiple members of the group, however, it takes plural verbs and pronouns.

> The audience <u>park their</u> cars in a new underground garage.
> Today the quartet <u>get their</u> paychecks.

college-application essay An ESSAY written as part of the application compiled for admission to colleges and universities.

While your college-application essay (or essays—some schools require several) will not be the only factor considered by an admissions committee, a poor essay may be enough to send your application into the reject pile. And a particularly strong piece of writing might well help the committee decide in your favor. Because this is such an important essay, give yourself every possible advantage by approaching the task wisely.

Members of the admissions committee hope to learn about you, both as a writer and as a person. They want to know if you are capable of doing college-level writing, and they want to know if you will add productively to the college community you hope to join. You need to put your best foot forward. Be honest. Be interesting. Present those sides of your character and experience that set you apart from your peers.

However, resist trying to be so unusual that your application appears cute or silly. Stories abound of applicants sending the committee homemade cookies, video presentations, and balloon bouquets. As inventive as these attempts are, they typically haven't worked.

Approach the task as you would any important writing assignment. Good writing takes time. Give yourself plenty. Use several PREWRITING strategies (BRAINSTORMING, CLUSTERING, FREEWRITING, LISTING, LOOPING,

See also
APPLICATION, LETTER
OF
LETTER, BUSINESS

MAPPING) to generate lots of ideas. Analyze the writing assignment and identify a FOCUS that fits.

Put away your draft (see DRAFTING) for a few days. You will then be able to review it more critically. Does it respond to the assignment? Is it clearly organized? What else do your readers need to know? What extraneous information should you eliminate? Get lots of feedback. Ask family, friends, and teachers to give you responses to your draft (see CONFERENCING).

Edit rigorously (see EDITING). Get help if you are not a good editor. This essay must be perfect.

Type your essay. You may be able to print it from a computer onto the application form. If not, you can print it to fit the available space and then cut and paste it in. This is not the place for fancy fonts; stick with something safe such as Times Roman or Arial.

Take extra care in putting the ADDRESS on the envelope. Print or type the address, and make sure your FORMAT is correct. Include a return address. Check the postage.

Mail your essay in plenty of time. Some schools are quite particular about their deadlines. You don't want to find yourself rejected because your hard work arrived a day or two late.

Net Source

Visit the College Board at <www.collegeboard.org>.

College Board The organization best known for administering the SAT and PSAT (formerly known as the Scholastic Aptitude Test and the Preliminary Scholastic Aptitude Test), the College-Level Examination Program (CLEP), and the Advanced Placement Program (AP). The board is an association of schools, colleges, and other educational institutions dedicated to helping people go to college. It offers a variety of programs and services related to college information and applications, college credit, and financial aid for college.

colloquialism INFORMAL words and PHRASES used in conversational language. Colloquialisms are not as informal as SLANG.

COLLOQUIALISM	MEANING
fixing to	getting ready to
he goes	he said
I'm like	I said
get cracking	hurry

Colloquialisms may reduce the effectiveness of your writing because readers may not understand you or may not take you seriously.

colon The PUNCTUATION mark : used to introduce explanations, examples, and QUOTATIONS and to separate parts of written expressions.

A colon may introduce a LIST.

Use the three primary colors: red, yellow, and blue.

Do not use a colon to separate a VERB and its COMPLEMENT unless it is a quotation.

The primary colors are: red, yellow, and blue.
He said: "The king is dead. Long live the king."

A colon may introduce a quotation after a complete sentence.

A line from Walt Whitman's *Song of Myself* illustrates paradox: "My faith is the greatest of faiths and the least of faiths" (line 1097).

A colon may introduce a related idea or an example.

You need not rinse the paintbrush between applications: simply begin with the lightest shade, and work toward the darkest.

Punctuation Pointer

Do not put a colloquialism in QUOTATION MARKS. The marks imply that you are apologizing for using the term.

Our trip was far-out.

See also
BIBLE, CITING
BIBLIOGRAPHY

Punctuation Pointer

When an INDEPENDENT CLAUSE follows a colon, some teachers require a capital letter, while some prefer a lowercased first word.

Students' needs vary: Some require ten hours of sleep, but some need only six.

Students' needs vary: some require ten hours of sleep, but some need only six.

The colon has many uses as a mark of separation:

10:15 A.M. [colon to separate hours and minutes]

Genesis 1:1 [colon to separate chapter and verse in biblical reference]

Dear Sir or Madam: [colon to separate SALUTATION and body of business LETTER]

Studies in Philosophy: A Collection of Essays [colon to separate book TITLE and SUBTITLE]

New York: Knopf [colon to separate place of publication from publisher in a bibliographical entry]

combining form A linguistic form that occurs only in **compounds,** words that may consist of a combination of ROOTS, AFFIXES, and other combining forms. For example, in English the form *tele* never stands on its own; it is always part of a compound such as *telephone, telegraph,* or *television,* and so it may be labeled a combining form. Similarly, the combining form *phil* appears not on its own but only in words such as *philharmonic* and *bibliophile.* Some dictionaries and textbooks may designate a particular word part as a combining form, while others may label it an affix (PREFIX or SUFFIX) or root. Both classification systems are acceptable.

combining sentences *See* SENTENCE COMBINING

See also
FARCE
HUMOR
IRONY
ROMANCE
SATIRE

comedy A literary work that aims to amuse its AUDIENCE. Comedies range from those that offer one joke after another to more subtle works that focus on a CHARACTER or characters who resolve a problem and gain a better state of mind or sense of self.

Many people use the term *comedy* to refer specifically to THEATER, movies, and television programs, but it can also be applied to other forms, such as SHORT STORIES and NOVELS, as well.

In classical DRAMA—including ancient Greek and Latin works as well as the plays of Shakespeare and eighteenth-century French writers—comedy ends happily and deals with ordinary people, unlike TRAGEDY, which ends unhappily and deals with idealized people.

comma *See p. 62*

comma fault *See* COMMA SPLICE

command *See* IMPERATIVE SENTENCE; SENTENCE

comma splice PUNCTUATION error in which two or more INDEPENDENT CLAUSES, each of which could stand alone as a SENTENCE, are joined with only a COMMA.

> The soccer ball bounced across the street, the children ran after it.

Repair a comma splice in one of the following ways:
- Let each independent clause stand alone as a sentence.

  > The soccer ball bounced across the street. The children ran after it.

- Insert a coordinate CONJUNCTION after the comma.

  > The soccer ball bounced across the street, and the children ran after it.

(continues on p. 67)

The two faces of theater: comedy (left) and tragedy (right)

See also
RUN-ON SENTENCE

COMMA A mark of PUNCTUATION mainly used to separate elements of a SENTENCE. Commas often correspond to pauses in speech (but not always, so don't rely on that cue to decide when to put a comma in your writing). A better approach is to learn the rules that apply to comma placement.

Easy Comma Rules: The Conventions

Always use the comma in the following situations:

1. Around the year in complete dates and around the state in city-state references (and in other similar references)

   December 7, 1941, is the date Pearl Harbor was attacked. [*But note that there is no comma in* "December 1941 seems long ago."]

   Cleveland, Ohio, is the home of several major corporations. [*But note that there is no comma after the state in* "My address ends with New York, NY 10024."]

   Read Act III, scenes 1–3, for homework.

2. After the SALUTATION of an informal letter (see LETTER, FRIENDLY)

   Dear Laurie,

   The salutation of a business letter is followed by a COLON.

3. After the CLOSING of a letter

   Sincerely yours,

4. With titles after names

   Joyce Brothers, Ph.D.

Lee Iacocca, former president of Chrysler,
   spoke at the convention.

5. Before QUOTATIONS

Franklin Delano Roosevelt said, "The only thing
we have to fear is fear itself."

You may use a colon if the quotation is longer
than one sentence.

    Do not use a comma with an INDIRECT
QUOTATION.

Roosevelt said that the only thing we have to
fear is fear itself.

Commas with Individual Words

6. Use commas around DIRECT ADDRESS.

I didn't say that, Mom.
I wrote the essay, Mr. Sanchez, but I forgot to
   bring it with me.

7. Use a comma after an introductory MODIFIER.

Thankfully, the rain ended.

Commas with Phrases

8. Use a comma between **coordinate adjectives**
before a NOUN.

It was a cold, cloudy night.

Adjectives are coordinate if they modify the
noun to an equal degree. Their order can be
changed, or *and* can be placed between them,
and the sentence will still sound correct.

Commas would not be correct in a sentence such as "He refinished the big old oak desk."

9. Use commas around an antithetical phrase (see ANTITHESIS).

Des Moines, not Dubuque, is the capital of Iowa.

10. Use commas around a NONRESTRICTIVE APPOSITIVE.

Kathy, my older sister, attends college.

11. Use commas with sentence interrupters and PARENTHETICAL EXPRESSIONS.

Wyoming, in fact, was the first state to allow women to vote.
Ohio, on the other hand, has been the home of several presidents.
He stood, thoroughly stunned, as the judge read the verdict.

12. Use a comma after some introductory expressions. Some writers, for example, use a comma after a sequence of two or more PREPOSITIONAL PHRASES.

Out of respect for the victims, the police delayed questioning them.
Rising to his feet, he bellowed.

Commas with Clauses

13. Use commas around nonrestrictive RELATIVE, or ADJECTIVE, CLAUSES.

My youngest brother, who works in New York City, visited over Christmas.

The Rocky Mountains, which extend from Mexico to Canada, include several different ranges.

14. Use commas to set off an introductory ADVERB CLAUSE or adverb clause that interrupts a **main clause.**

When the gong sounds, the game is over.
The game, although it lasted twelve innings, seemed short.

Use a comma with concluding adverb clauses if the information in the adverb clause contrasts with or contradicts the information in the INDEPENDENT CLAUSE. Otherwise, don't use a comma before a concluding adverb clause.

The game seemed short, although it lasted twelve innings.
The game seemed short because the day was so pleasant.

15. Use a comma between the clauses of a **compound sentence** unless the clauses are short and the meaning is still clear.

The suspects fled the scene, and the police followed them.

The Series Comma

16. Use a comma to separate items in a series. The comma between the last two items in a series is optional but preferred.

We took flashlights, tents, a cookstove, and our fishing gear.

Misuses of the Comma

17. Do not use commas between parts of a COM-POUND SUBJECT or COMPOUND VERB.

The boy,⁄ and his sister went to the movies.
The boy and his sister went to the movies,⁄and
   then ate dinner.

The second sentence can also be corrected by giving the verb *ate* its own SUBJECT, making a compound sentence: "The boy and his sister went to the movies, and then <u>they</u> ate dinner."

18. Do not rely on a comma alone to link independent clauses, or you will create a COMMA SPLICE. Use a SEMICOLON, write two complete sentences, or add a coordinate CONJUNCTION after the comma.

The dog chased the cat,⁄the cat turned and
   hissed at him.
Pat was class valedictorian,⁄however, she decided not to attend college.

19. Do not use a comma between a SUBJECT and its VERB or between a verb and its COMPLEMENT.

That the space shuttle exploded,⁄was a tragedy.
Some people do not know,⁄that the Nile River
   flows to the north.

20. Do not use a comma before the first or after the final item in a series.

I asked for,⁄clothes, money, and books,⁄for my
birthday.

(continued from p. 61)

- Replace the comma with a SEMICOLON or, if appropriate, a COLON.

  > The soccer ball bounced across the street; the children ran after it.

- Replace the comma with a semicolon plus a conjunctive ADVERB and a comma.

  > The soccer ball bounced across the street; <u>consequently</u>, the children ran after it.

- Subordinate one clause to the other (see SUBORDINATION).

  > When the soccer ball bounced across the street, the children ran after it.

> **— Helpful Hint —**
>
> You will certainly see comma splices in print. Advertisers, in particular, tend to use them. The British are also more likely than Americans to use comma splices. Most style guides do allow for extremely short independent clauses to be joined by a comma.
>
> I came, I saw, I conquered.
>
> Nevertheless, generally avoid comma splices in your writing.

commendation, letter of A letter expressing appreciation for a favor or complimenting a person, group, or organization on a job well done. More formal than a personal THANK-YOU LETTER, a letter of commendation uses a business letter format (see LETTER, BUSINESS).

Each of the following possibilities calls for a letter expressing your gratitude: a business person has allowed you to interview company personnel as part of a school project; your creative writing class has visited a nearby grade school to read the children's books you had written for the first-grade class; several parents have helped you with your job fair, bringing professional materials and meeting with interested students; your school service club has heard a particularly outstanding speaker.

The key to writing a good letter of commendation is sincerity. Don't let your letter sound like a form letter, or it will lose its impact. Make sure you include particu-

lars—the specific items or services for which you are grateful or which have impressed you. Success depends on the generosity of others. In return, your words need to express your honest gratitude.

common noun A common noun names any one or more of a group of persons, places, things, or ideas. A PROPER NOUN names a particular person, place, thing, or idea.

> COMMON NOUNS: boy, dog, wall, building
>
> PROPER NOUNS: Abdul, Rover, the Vietnam War Memorial, the Texas School Book Depository

Except at the beginning of a SENTENCE or in a TITLE, use a lowercase letter to begin a common noun.

communication, theory of Explanation of how messages are exchanged between and among living things.

Communication acts involve three elements: (1) the sender, (2) the receiver, and (3) the message. Often the relationships among these aspects are portrayed as a communication triangle. The triangle suggests that each part of the communication act is equal and that none can exist without the others. That is, if a person is alone and speaks, there may be sound, but, because there is no receiver, there is no communication.

Sometimes communication breaks down because the sender neglects the receiver. For example, if a person has never been sailing before, and the captain of the boat yells, "Stand by to come about!" the receiver may understand each word but not the message. A communication act can also fail when too little attention is paid to the message. Imagine getting a note from a friend that simply says, "I'll meet you in front of the theater at

---

Helpful Hint

Be Specific

Make your writing stronger by selecting a specific common noun rather than relying on a general common noun plus an adjective.

SAY	INSTEAD OF
kitten	young cat
lieutenant	low-ranking officer
adrenaline	stress hormone

---

seven." Unless you have discussed which theater, you are likely to wind up at the wrong place.

Contemporary theories of communication address issues such as NONVERBAL COMMUNICATION, mass communication, small-group communication, cultural influence on communication, and communication among animals and between animals and humans.

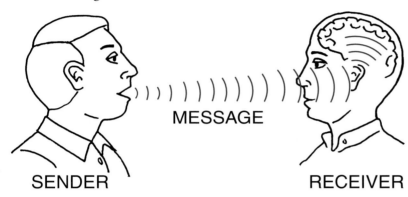

MESSAGE

SENDER   RECEIVER

comparative degree A form of ADJECTIVE or ADVERB that is used to compare two things. For adjectives of one SYLLABLE, some adjectives of two syllables, and adverbs without *ly*, generally form the comparative degree by adding the SUFFIX *er*. For some two-syllable adjectives, longer adjectives, and most adverbs, form the comparative degree by adding *more*.

See also
COMPARISON OF
MODIFIERS
SPELLING
SUPERLATIVE DEGREE

ADJECTIVE OR ADVERB	COMPARATIVE FORM
small	smaller
loud	louder
happy	happier
careful	more careful
colorful	more colorful
slowly	more slowly
frequently	more frequently

To indicate a lesser degree, the comparative form takes *less* before an adjective or an adverb: *less happy, less careful, less colorful, less slowly, less frequently.*

Some comparative forms are irregular (see IRREGULAR COMPARISON).

ADJECTIVE OR ADVERB	COMPARATIVE FORM
good, well	better
bad, badly	worse
little (quantity)	less
many, much	more

compare to/compare with Reserve *compare to* for instances in which you see a likeness between two *different* things.

> Shakespeare wrote, "Shall I compare thee to a summer's day?"
>
> I might compare my vacation experience to the hardships of the pioneers.

Use *compare with* when you compare two things of the same class or when you want to rank them.

> How do the Dartmouth students compare with those at Harvard?
>
> Compared with chocolate, vanilla finishes second.

See also
COMPARISON FRAME
ESSAY

comparison/contrast A method of DEVELOPMENT and an organizational pattern based on the relationships between two things; commonly used in EXPOSITION, writing that explains. This form of ANALYSIS is particularly useful when trying to show (1) the essential sameness between two apparently dissimilar things (how school and vacations are alike); (2) the essential differences between two apparently similar things (such as tourists and travelers); (3) the distinctions between apparently similar abstract terms, ideas, or attitudes (the differences between education and training, for example); or (4) the superiority of one thing over another, similar item. Comparison/contrast is also useful when analyzing a literary CHARACTER, particularly when the author has provided a FOIL.

When using comparison/contrast, keep your PURPOSE in mind; it is not enough to say, "X and Y are similar in these ways and different in these ways." The similarities and differences you highlight should serve to provide readers with new understanding. In the example that follows, the writer reminds readers that *discipline* and *punishment* are quite different, even though they may feel similar to the recipients at times.

Model

> Discipline is a training that develops self-control, character, or orderliness and efficiency. It does not necessarily call for a harsh penalty. Discipline may be enforced by parents, employers, and athletic coaches so that a child, employee, or athlete may learn the right rules and follow them.
>
> Punishment is a penalty imposed on an offender for a crime or wrongdoing. Punishment is usually harsh so that those who are deserving of it learn from their mistakes.

There are three methods of organizing comparison/contrast information: you might discuss all the similarities and then all the differences; you might discuss the two items, feature by feature, identifying and evaluating characteristics, or features, of each item; you might dis-

Checklist

WRITING A
COMPARISON/CONTRAST

1. Make a list of the features of each character or item in turn. For a character think about appearance, behavior, background, and speech; for a thing think about cost, size, value, and function. Be certain to examine the same features of the two characters or items.

2. Use your lists to answer two questions: How is X similar to Y? How is X different from Y? You may wish to use a VENN DIAGRAM or COMPARISON FRAME.

3. To determine your purpose, ask yourself, "What do I intend to show through the process of comparing and contrasting these two things?"

4. From your comparison/contrast lists choose features that fit your purpose.

cuss the items subject by subject, talking about all the features of one before discussing the other.

Assume that you are writing about tape cassettes and CDs. Here's an example of what each organizational method might look like:

Similarities, differences

Tape cassettes and CDs are both wonderfully portable, traveling to the library or beach with ease. Both can be listened to privately without disturbing others. Both provide a large range of music from heavy metal to country to classical. However, quality of sound and durability make CDs the choice of any discerning listener. Tape recordings simply cannot offer the resonance and depth of sound available on a CD. And CDs are hard to damage. Accidentally leaving one in the car on an August afternoon won't turn it into a sticky mass, as can happen with even a high-quality tape.

Feature by feature

On the issue of portability, neither cassettes nor CDs offer an advantage; both are eminently portable. But if you're concerned about cost, you may lean toward cassettes, which generally run a few dollars less than the same album on disc, and a tape player still costs less than a CD player. On the other hand, when handled according to directions, CDs may last longer than cassettes because no part of the music system actually touches the disc. Perhaps CDs are a better investment, after all.

Subject by subject

> Cassettes have been around a long time for three very good reasons. Cassettes are easy to transport; cassettes and cassette players are economical; and although the tape can become tangled or tear, cassettes can last a long time if handled well. However, CDs are also easily portable, if more expensive than cassettes, and may ultimately be a better investment because there's less chance that they will wear out from overuse.

comparison frame A **graphic organizer** that is useful during PREWRITING when you are developing material for COMPARISON/CONTRAST. Once you have decided (or been told) what to examine for similarities and differences, you need to list the features on which you will evaluate the two CHARACTERS or items, and then narrow down the features to those that will be most meaningful for your particular AUDIENCE and PURPOSE.

Suppose you were writing about CDs and cassette tapes. Your BRAINSTORMING might generate the following list of features.

portability
cost
durability
sound quality
storage
music selection
availability

Narrowing your list, you might decide to concentrate on portability, cost, durability, and sound quality. You would

See also
CHART
FLOW CHART
K-W-L CHART
VENN DIAGRAM

then analyze cassettes and CDs relative to each feature, and determine whether they are the same or different.

Similarities and Differences in Music Recordings			
	Cassette	Compact Disc	Same or Different?
PORTABILITY	easy to carry	easy to carry but surface must be protected	more similar than different
COST	average around $10	average around $15	different
DURABILITY	subject to tears, tangling, heat damage	subject to scratches	similar: both have problems
SOUND QUALITY	acceptable compared to vinyl	richer sound	different

Using the frame, you could then proceed to DRAFT your comparison/contrast.

comparison of modifiers Most MODIFIERS—ADJECTIVES and ADVERBS—have three different forms, called degrees of comparison. The three degrees are **positive degree,** COMPARATIVE DEGREE, and SUPERLATIVE DEGREE. Positive degree is the basic form of the word; do not use it to make a comparison.

The engine is <u>loud</u>.

The comparative degree goes beyond the positive degree to describe more of the same quality than the positive degree.

The engine is <u>louder</u> today than yesterday.

The superlative degree singles out the modified word.

> This is the <u>loudest</u> engine in the garage.

There are different ways to form comparisons, depending on the words used. Comparative degree is most often formed by adding *er* to the modifier, while superlative degree is most often formed by adding *est* to the modifier.

However, some words do not lend themselves to this formation, and the comparative degrees are formed instead by adding the modifiers *more* or *most*. These are often words whose positive-degree form already contains a SUFFIX.

> Of the two, Todd was <u>more careful</u>, but Patrick worked <u>more efficiently</u>.

The different comparison forms—*er* and *more; est* and *most*—are alternatives and may not be used together. Only one comparison form, the correct one for the word, should be used. Thus it is incorrect to say *more happier;* such an expression is called a **double comparison**. Only the correct form, *happier,* may be used for comparison.

Irregular Comparison

Other words have irregular comparison forms, in that their comparatives are formed by using entirely different words. Some examples include *good (better, best); bad (worse, worst);* and *many (more, most).*

Decreasing Comparison

Decreasing comparisons are always formed by adding the terms *less* or *least* to the modifier.

I am <u>less happy</u> at work than on vacation, but I am <u>least happy</u> at the doctor's office.

Illogical and Incomplete Comparisons

Some words, by their very definition, are in a sense superlatives; they do not allow for any qualification by degrees. These words include *unique, equal, infinite,* or *empty.* An attempt at comparison of these terms is illogical because it undermines the meaning of the word. Therefore, do not write or say "most unique" or "emptier."

Avoid incomplete comparisons by ensuring that when a comparative modifier is used, the SENTENCE contains another term for comparison.

> INCOMPLETE: It was more economical to rent a car.
> CORRECTED: It was more economical to rent a car than to buy one.

When you are comparing one member of a group with the group as a whole, you must include the word *other* or *else* to make the comparison complete.

> She is smarter than anyone <u>else</u>.

When making a comparison, be sure you are comparing like items or equal parts of the sentence.

> ILLOGICAL: The map of Australia shows more desert than the United States.

In this example, *map* is illogically compared to *United States.* A corrected version would either compare two maps or two countries:

> The map of Australia shows more desert than the map of the United States.
> Australia has more desert than the United States has.

complaint, letter of *See* ADJUSTMENT, LETTER OF

complement A grammatical element that completes the meaning of a VERB or another complement. (Note: not all verbs need or have a complement.) *Complement* is the general name given to the completers, also called DIRECT OBJECT, INDIRECT OBJECT, OBJECT COMPLEMENT, and SUBJECT COMPLEMENT. Complements can be single words, PHRASES, or CLAUSES.

A direct object answers the question *what?* or *whom?* after an action verb.

> The artist created <u>a mural</u>.

Here the direct object after *created* answers the question *what?*

An indirect object answers the question *to what?, to whom?, for what?,* or *for whom?* after an ACTION VERB.

> Show <u>me</u> your new car.

Here the indirect object after the verb *show* answers the question *to whom?* The example also shows that more than one complement can occur in a sentence, since *your new car* is also a complement—a direct object.

An object complement answers the question *what?* after a direct object. It completes the meaning of the direct object by identifying or describing it. Object complements occur with a limited number of verbs that have the general meaning "make" or "consider," including *call, consider, find, make, name, prove, think,* and others.

> Architects find plans <u>essential</u>.
> We named our dog <u>Goofy</u>.

Helpful Hint

It's *I* or *It's me*?
When you're talking with your friends, it's OK to say "It's me." But when you are speaking or writing in a more FORMAL situation, the appropriate complement after "It's" is "I."

A subject complement follows a SUBJECT and a LINKING VERB and identifies or describes the subject. Subject complements are of two sorts: a PREDICATE NOMINATIVE follows a linking verb and points back to the subject to identify it.

> Teachers are <u>people</u>, too.

A PREDICATE ADJECTIVE follows a linking verb, points back to the subject, and further describes it.

> Teachers are <u>creative</u>.

complement/compliment *Complement* as a VERB means "to go with" or "to complete" and as a NOUN means "either of two parts that complete each other." *Compliment* as a verb means "to speak or behave admiringly" and as a noun refers to a remark that indicates admiration.

> The colors of your furniture <u>complement</u> your new rug.
> A *B* was the highest <u>compliment</u> Professor Higgenbotham had ever paid a student.

complete predicate *See* PREDICATE

complete subject *See* SUBJECT

complex sentence *See* SENTENCE

complications In a NARRATIVE or dramatic PLOT the difficult circumstances that must be worked out by a CHARACTER who faces a CONFLICT. Complications can be physical (a shipwreck, stolen evidence, a missing witness) or psychological (the hero's love for a woman he believes may

---

Memory Jogger

I receive a compl**i**ment.
Compl**e**mentary angles fit together.

---

be the murderer, a parent's favoring one child over another). A writer who manages complications well creates a RESOLUTION that is logical and believable, emerging naturally as the tale unfolds.

compose/comprise Both verbs indicate the makeup of something. Parts *compose* a whole; the whole *comprises* the parts.

> The president, vice president, secretary, treasurer, and a representative from each homeroom <u>compose</u> the student council.
>
> The student council <u>comprises</u> the president, vice president, secretary, treasurer, and a representative from each homeroom.

composition *See* ESSAY; WRITING, KINDS OF

compound *See* COMBINING FORM

compound adjective A multiword ADJECTIVE that may appear before or after the NOUN.

> We took the <u>crosstown</u> bus to the museum.
> We went to the <u>first-floor</u> exhibits.
> They included <u>computer-enhanced</u> dioramas.
> The exhibits were <u>well attended</u>.

Write a compound adjective before a noun as a closed-up word if it appears as such in your DICTIONARY (as in the first example), but hyphenate most other compound adjectives before a noun (as in the second and third examples). In general, do not hyphenate compound adjectives that appear after the noun (as in the fourth example).

Helpful Hint

Compose/Comprise
Avoid using the passive *is composed of* or *is comprised of.*

Punctuation Pointer

Do not hyphenate a compound modifier made from an *ly* adverb and an adjective.

Here's a <u>clearly marked</u> exit.

Notice how a HYPHEN can clarify your meaning.

We use plants as living room decoration.
We use plants as living-room decoration.

compound-complex sentence *See* SENTENCE

compound noun
A multiword NOUN. Consult a DICTIONARY or style guide to determine whether a compound noun should be closed up, hyphenated, or left open (with a space between words).

> houseboat, great-grandmother, high school, editor in chief, Latin America

compound predicate *See* COMPOUND VERB

compound preposition
A two- or three-word PREPOSITION, which shows the relationship between a NOUN or PRONOUN and another word.

Most commonly used prepositions consist of a single word such as *in, by, to, above, with,* or *of.* Common examples of compound prepositions include

according to	in front of
ahead of	in spite of
along with	instead of
apart from	next to
aside from	on account of
as to	on top of
because of	out of
by means of	owing to
in addition to	

We stayed home <u>because of</u> the bad weather.
We went on a picnic <u>in spite of</u> the bad weather.

— Helpful Hint — 👉

Compound Noun? Or Adjective + Noun?
Peanut butter is a compound noun; without *peanut* the word *butter* calls a different food to mind. But *whipped butter* is not a compound noun; with or without *whipped* you picture the same food. *Whipped butter* is simply an ADJECTIVE plus a noun.

---

compound sentence *See* COMMA; CONJUNCTION; MONOTONY, AVOIDING; SEMICOLON; SENTENCE

compound subject Two or more SUBJECTS joined by a CONJUNCTION and having the same VERB or verbs.

The conjunction most often used to join subjects is *and*.

> The <u>man</u> and the <u>woman</u> went to the movies and ate dinner afterward.

Notice that the compound subject in the example takes a PLURAL verb.

A correlative CONJUNCTION can also join subjects.

> Neither <u>the dog</u> nor <u>the cat</u> is sleeping right now.

Notice that in the example sentence, in which both the subjects are SINGULAR, the verb is singular. But if the subject nearer the verb is plural, then the verb is also plural.

> Neither the <u>dog</u> nor the <u>cats</u> are sleeping.

compound verb Two or more VERBS or VERB PHRASES joined by a CONJUNCTION and having the same SUBJECT.

> The performer <u>danced</u> and <u>sang</u>.
> The performer <u>can't dance</u> but <u>can sing</u>.

When an AUXILIARY VERB is used in a compound verb, the auxiliary is often not repeated.

> The performer <u>will dance, sing</u>, and <u>play</u> the piano.

A compound verb is not the same as a COMPOUND SENTENCE, which has two or more INDEPENDENT CLAUSES, each with its own subject.

See also
AGREEMENT,
SUBJECT-VERB

> ## Punctuation Pointer
>
> When more than two subjects make up a compound subject, separate them with COMMAS and use the conjunction only between the last two.
>
> <u>Eggs, cheese,</u> and <u>ham</u> combine to make a delicious omelette.

computer *See p. 84*

The performer danced, and

the accompanist played the piano.

computer *See p. 84*

computer catalog *See* CATALOG, LIBRARY

conceit An extended METAPHOR in which two strikingly different things are likened. Popular with English poets of the sixteenth and seventeenth centuries (such as Shakespeare and John Donne), the conceit originated in Italy and was common in love sonnets by the Italian poet Petrarch.

Some readers think a conceit can be ineffective or strained. For example, some argue that the sixteenth-century poem "My Galley" by Sir Thomas Wyatt goes too far in comparing the forlorn lover to a ship tossed about at sea.

conciseness in writing The opposite of WORDINESS, conciseness is the quality that makes PROSE direct and well crafted. When EDITING, look for ways to make your writing concise without sacrificing meaning or important DETAIL. You may find the following strategies helpful.

1. **Eliminate REDUNDANCY.** PHRASES such as *true fact, redid again,* and *thought in his mind* are redundant.
2. **Eliminate empty words.** Often you can omit ARTICLES (*the, a,* and *an*) with no loss of meaning. A stronger ADJECTIVE or ADVERB can replace an INTENSIFIER such as *very, really,* or *terribly.*
3. **Sharpen your VERBS.** Replace a verb and MODIFIER (*ran quickly*) with a strong verb (*raced*). Simple past, present, and future TENSES generally convey

---

Punctuation Pointer

In general, do not use a comma to separate a compound verb made up of only two verbs.

The performer danced/and sang.

But if someone might misread your prose, do use a comma.

He closed his eyes**,** and screamed.

Without the comma the reader might expect another DIRECT OBJECT, as in "He closed his eyes and mouth."

the necessary information and are more direct (and easier to follow) than the PERFECT TENSES ("He went" instead of "He had gone").

4. **Eliminate DEADWOOD.** Rewrite SENTENCES that begin *There is* or *It was;* make them more direct. Cut phrases such as *in my opinion, for the most part,* and *last but not least,* which add little to your meaning.

conclusion (of essay) The final SENTENCE or PARAGRAPH that brings closure to an ESSAY. Probably the most difficult part of an essay to write, the conclusion is also the most important part as the ideas it presents are the ones readers leave with.

Writers use a variety of strategies to create a strong conclusion.

1. **Summarize.** Although functional, SUMMARY isn't terribly interesting, especially for the conclusion of a short essay where it often feels repetitive.

2. **Loop back to the beginning.** Reread your INTRODUCTION. Is there an element there—an image, an ANECDOTE, a DESCRIPTION, a QUOTATION—that you can mention again in the conclusion?

3. **Tell a story.** Use a brief ANECDOTE that illustrates the point(s) you have been making.

4. **Use a quotation.** This might be from an authority, underscoring your point, or it might simply be a statement that is powerful because of its authenticity.

5. **Ask a question.** Leave readers with something new to think about based on the information you have presented so far.

Helpful Hint

What to Avoid
Writers sometimes use PHRASES such as "In conclusion," "Finally," or "To summarize" to signal the conclusion of the essay. Because they are overused, these phrases can sound formulaic and boring. Use the strategies mentioned in the entry to provide a memorable close.

COMPUTER Computers have capabilities that far surpass any previous writing, research, or printing technology. They allow you to have quick, easy access to a wide variety of research material through the INTERNET; to draft and revise documents through the use of word-processing programs; to create CHARTS, TABLES, and other graphics that make documents more interesting and easier to understand; and to produce multiple copies of professional-looking documents through the use of desktop-publishing capabilities.

Computers are composed of two distinct parts: hardware and software. Hardware is the equipment itself: the computer, printer, cables, keyboard, and so on. Software refers to the programming that allows the computer to perform. Software can be added to, changed, or removed from a computer system.

The Internet and Learning from Documents

The Internet is a set, or network, of connections between computers through telephone lines and other means. Because computers can exchange information, anyone with a computer can research a topic by connecting with the computer at the source of the information. Instead of connecting by a telephone number, however, the connection is made by typing in an "address" of the information source.

These addresses, known as Uniform Resource Locators (URLs), identify specific and unique sources of information in the Internet network. These sources are commonly referred to as Web sites, a term that derives from the computer programming and telephone-line system that connects all these addresses, the WORLD WIDE WEB.

The Internet provides tremendous research possibilities because it also allows you to perform searches on general topics when you don't have a specific address. SEARCH ENGINES are tools you can use to type in KEYWORDS about the topic being researched (see BOOLEAN SEARCH). The search engine quickly scans through the addresses in the system to provide a list of those that may include the information that you have requested.

Many individuals, news organizations, businesses, schools, universities, museums, libraries, and research organizations from around the world provide Web sites with information—often including pictures, sound, or video—on a vast array of topics on the Internet. Whenever you are using any of these Internet research tools, you may accidentally link to a Web site that contains something offensive. Exit such a site immediately, and inform a parent, teacher, librarian, or other supervisor about the offensive site.

The Internet and Learning from Discussion

The Internet also lets you talk to other Internet users, who can be a valuable source of information. One way to interact is through *listservs,* which allow you to ask a question of a group of people who post messages about a specific topic. You can also take part in discussion groups in which people with knowledge about a particular topic hold "discussions" by typing their comments on the screen. Similarly, you can interview experts on a topic by sending them questions and getting responses through E-MAIL. The Internet also allows you to take classes long-distance by corresponding over the Internet with an instructor and other students in different locations.

Challenging and Citing the Internet

When you locate material through an Internet Web site, you must evaluate its accuracy and validity. Look at the last time the site was updated. If it has not been updated recently, you may wonder if the people who created the site are responsible; perhaps their material is not trustworthy. In addition, look at the name of the group who created the site, and determine whether the group might have any reason to give biased information. If you think the information may be biased, you should find a site that contains a different viewpoint. Comparing viewpoints can be a useful research tool. Certainly relying on one viewpoint only is not good research.

If you then use the material in a RESEARCH PAPER or ORAL PRESENTATION, you must document the source just as you document books and periodicals (see DOCUMENTATION).

Word-Processing and Presentation Programs

Word-processing programs have tools that help you in EDITING your drafts. For example, they may allow you or another reader to place a vertical line next to SENTENCES or passages that need revision.

Word-processing programs also usually contain a SPELL CHECKER and grammar checker. The spell-checking tool identifies misspelled words but cannot tell you when you have, for instance, typed *you* instead of *your*. Similarly, the grammar-checking program can alert you to some basic problems but not to everything. Therefore, you should never simply rely on these programs instead of reading through your work yourself.

In the past the creation of BOLDFACE TYPE, ITALICS, and **footnotes** was cumbersome if not impossible on a typewriter or in handwritten work. Today word-processing programs allow you to put real italic and bold type in your documents. These programs also allow you to insert footnotes, with the program automatically adjusting the page length to accommodate the footnotes.

Word-processing programs also allow you great flexibility in the look of a document—its margins, the space between lines and PARAGRAPHS, and the use of columns (see FORMAT).

Most word-processing programs contain some graphics options that allow you to add TABLES, CHARTS, and GRAPHS, such as PIE CHARTS or BAR GRAPHS, and to create drawings and insert SYMBOLS into a document. Writers who have access to presentation programs such as Power Point usually have even more illustration options and, with the right hookups, can give oral presentations with accompanying visual aids projected right from the computer onto a screen.

These capabilities mean that a writer can produce a professional, printed document or presentation without any equipment other than a computer and printer. This process has come to be known as desktop publishing. Word-processing programs enable the user to select from a wide variety of print styles and sizes, to create covers, captions, headings, and other aspects of a final printed product that were not formerly available except with large, expensive printing equipment.

concrete noun A NOUN that names something that can be recognized by the senses. Examples include *tree, desk, baby,* and *building*. In contrast to a concrete noun is an ABSTRACT NOUN, which names an idea, concept, quality, or state: *kindness, love, success, thought.*

conditional expression An expression beginning with *if* or its equivalent.

> If Mary goes, John will go.
> As long as I get a paycheck, I'll work.

Conditional expressions are often hypothetical, or contrary to the truth, so you sometimes have to use the SUBJUNCTIVE MOOD.

> If I were you [but I'm not], I would do my homework first.
> If Mary were to go, John would go.

conferencing Getting feedback about writing to help with REVISING and EDITING.

A revision conference can be as informal as handing a friend or an instructor a copy of your draft and asking for a response, or it can be as formal as following a set of steps your teacher requires of you in class. Formal or informal, with friends or an instructor, the purpose of conferencing is to get information that will help you make your writing more interesting and more effective.

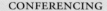

Checklist

CONFERENCING

1. Don't explain or apologize for your piece.
2. Take detailed notes that you can return to later.
3. Get feedback from several readers.

Set Index

Bold numerals refer to volume numbers. *Italic* volume and page numbers indicate where main entries can be found. Most entries in capital letters signify the building-block terms considered most important for language-arts students. The words in bold identify the eleven categories into which the more than one thousand entries fall. Following each bold term are some of its representative main entries.

oral literature, **1:** 29, *7: 15–16*

oral presentation, **2:** 5, 6–7, **4:** 35, *7: 16–17*

oral/verbal, 7: 18

order (in writing), **1:** 20, *7: 18,* 31, **9:** 13, **10:** 81

ordinal number, *7: 18*

organization, name of, **1:** 55, **2:** 15–16, 22, 24, **4:** 80, *7: 20*

organization (of writing), *7: 20*

orthography. *See* spelling

OUTLINE, **6:** 87, *7: 22–23*

outside of, 7: 20

overgeneralization, *7: 20–21*

overstatement, *7: 21*

owing to the fact that, 7: 21

oxymoron, *7: 24*

panel discussion, **6:** 44, *7: 25*

pantomime, *7: 25–26*

paper. *See* book report; five-paragraph essay; research paper; thesis statement

parable, *7: 26*

paradox, *7: 26*

PARAGRAPH, *7: 28–29*

parallelism, **3:** 16, *7: 26–27*

paraphrase, **6:** 75, *7: 27, 32,* 60

parentheses, **3:** 22, **6:** 32, *7: 32–34,* **8:** 22

  with brackets, **2:** 10, **8:** 18, 19

  with other punctuation, **3:** 68–69, *7: 33–34,* 43, **8:** 26

parenthetical documentation, **3:** 64–65, 66, *7: 34*

parenthetical expression, **2:** 64, *7: 34*

parody, *7: 34*

participial phrase, *7: 34–35,* **10:** 54

participle, *7: 35–36*

parts of a sentence, *9: 11–13*

PARTS OF SPEECH, *7: 38–39*

Parts of Speech. *See* adjective, adverb, conjunction, interjection, noun, preposition, pronoun, verb

pass., 5: 80

passive voice, **1:** 13, *7: 36–37,* **10:** 64–67

pastoral, 7: 37

past participle, **5:** 59–63, *7: 37*

past perfect, overuse of, **10:** 11, 12

past-perfect tense, **5:** 60, *7: 37,* 40, **10:** 10

past progressive, *7:* 87

past tense, **5:** 59–63, *7: 40,* **10:** 9

peer editing, peer response, *7: 40,* **10:** 83

pen name, *7: 41*

pentameter, **5:** 18

people/persons, 7: 41

per, 7: 41

percent/percentage, 7: 41

perfect tenses. *See* future-perfect tense; past-perfect tense; present-perfect tense

performance assessment, *7: 42*

period, **6:** 29, *7: 42–43,* **8:** 21

periodical, **3:** 62, 66, **5:** 35, 87, *7: 44*

periodic sentence, *7: 43–44*

persecute/prosecute, 7: 45

person, *7: 45–47*

persona, *7: 47,* **9:** 45

personal expression, **10:** 78

personal narrative, *7: 48–49*

personally, 7: 47–48

personal/personnel, 7: 50

personal pronoun, *7: 50,* **8:** 6

personification, **5:** 23, *7: 50–51*

persuasion, **1:** 26, **6:** 15, *7: 52,* **10:** 45–46, 79

phoneme, *7: 52–53*

phonetic symbol, *7: 53*

PHRASE, **5:** 43–44, **6:** 46, *7: 34–35, 7: 56–57,* **10:** 54–55

picaresque novel, **6:** 80, *7: 54*

pictograph, **1:** 38–40, *7: 54–55*

pie chart (circle graph), **4:** 81, **4:** 86, *7: 55*

place names, *7: 58–59*

plagiarism, **3:** 63, **6:** 75, *7: 59–60*

planets, stars, heavenly bodies, *7: 58–59, 7: 61*

play. *See* drama

plot, **2:** 78–79, *7: 61–62*

plural, **4:** 14, **6:** 56, 78–79, *7: 63–64,* 70, 71

p.m. *or* P.M., **5:** 80

poetic device. *See* figurative language; sound effects

poetic form, *7: 65–66*

poetic license, *7: 64–65*

poetry, *7: 65–66*

point of view, **6:** 9, *7: 66–68,* **9:** 18

political term, capitalizing, **4:** 80, **8:** 14

poll, *7: 68*

portfolio, *7: 68–69*

portmanteau word, *7: 69*

Portuguese, **2:** 31, *7: 69*

positive degree, **2:** 74

possessive, **1:** 20, *7: 69–70*

possessive case, **2:** 26–27, **6:** 79, *7: 70–71*

possessive pronoun, **8:** 7

postal service abbreviations, **1:** 5, 14–15

post ergo hoc, 8: 37

practical writing. *See* E-mail; letter, business; memo

precede/proceed, 7: 71

précis. *See* paraphrase; summary

PREDICATE, *7: 72–74,* **9:** 12

predicate adjective, **2:** 78, *7: 75*

predicate noun (predicate nominative), **2:** 78, *7: 75–76*

predicting outcomes, *7: 76*

preface, **1:** 88, **6:** 88

prefix, **5:** 16, **6:** 40, *7: 76–78,* **9:** 49, **10:** 62, 74

premise. *See* reasoning

preposition, **4:** 13, *7: 39, 7: 79–80*

prepositional phrase, **1:** 17, 34, **2:** 64, *7: 56–57,* *7: 80*

present participle, **4:** 77, *7: 80*

present-perfect form of the infinitive, **5:** 43

present-perfect tense, **5:** 60, *7: 81,* **10:** 9–10

present progressive, *7:* 87

present tense, **5:** *12, 7: 81,* **10:** 8

press release, *7: 81*

pretty, 7: 81

prewriting, *7: 82,* **10:** 80–81

primary source, *7: 83*

principal parts of a verb, *7: 84,* **10:** 52–53

principal/principle, 7: 85

prior knowledge, building on, *7: 85*

problem-and-solution essay, *7: 85–86*

process, explaining a, *7: 86–87*

progressive forms of verbs, *7: 87,* **10:** 10–11

prologue, *7: 87–88*

PRONOUN, *7: 38,* **8:** 7–10

  See also agreement, pronoun-antecedent

pronunciation of words, **1:** 9, *7: 53*

proof, **3:** 38, **4:** 29

proofreading, **2:** 25, **8:** 5, *11, 12,* **10:** 83

propaganda, *8: 11*

proper adjective, **1:** 20, **8:** *12–13*

proper noun, **1:** 5–6, **2:** 21–24, **6:** 28, 55–56, 78, **8:** *13–14*

prose, **8:** *15*

protagonist, **6:** 21, **8:** *15*

proverb, **8:** *15*

PSAT/NMSQT, **8:** 81

pseudonym, *7:* 41

publishing, **8:** *15–16,* **9:** 17, **10:** 83–84

Pulitzer Prize, **8:** 16

pun, **8:** *16–17*

PUNCTUATION, **6:** 29–33, **8:** *18–23*

purple prose, **8:** *17*

purpose for writing, *7:* 82, **8:** *17,* **10:** 80

put, **5:** 20–21

quatrain, **8:** *24*

quest (archetype), **8:** *24–25*

question, **5:** 37, 52, 54, *7: 74*

question mark, **5:** 52, **6:** 29, **8:** 21–22, **8:** *25–26*

questionnaire, **8:** 26

quiet/quit/quite, 8: 27

quotation, **1:** 85, **5:** 38, 54, **6:** 75, **8:** *27–28*

quotation mark, **2:** 8, 59, **4:** 72, **8:** 22–23, **8:** *28–30*

quotations, book of, **8:** *30*

rain/reign/rein, 8: 31

raise/rise, 8: 31

reader-response criticism, **6:** 13

reader-response journal, **5:** *70–71*

Readers' Guide, **8:** *32*

readers' theater, *7:* 15, **8:** *32–33,* 68–69

reading, **8:** *33–35*

realism, **8:** *35–36*

real/very/really, 8: 36

reasoning, **3:** 30–31, **5:** 42, *7: 20–21,* **8:** *36–37,* **9:** 84

reason is because, 8: 38

reason why, 8: 38

reciprocal pronoun, **8:** 8, **8:** *38*

redundancy, **3:** 27, *7: 48,* **8:** *38–40*

refer/allude, 1: 37

reference, letter of, **8:** *40*

reference, pronoun. *See* agreement, pronoun-antecedent; pronoun

reference source, **8:** *40–41*

reflecting, **8:** *42,* **10:** 84

reflexive pronoun, **5:** 24, **8:** 7, **8:** *42*

refrain, **2:** 41–42, **8:** *42*